# English
# Olympiad

## Class 10

**A must have book for all
Olympiads & Talent Search Exams...**

*by*
Vaishali Sharma

**BLoOM** CAP
**Bloom Cap Edu Ventures Pvt. Ltd.**

## Bloom Cap Edu Ventures Pvt. Ltd.




ॐ **Administrative & Production Office**

'Ramchhaya' 4577/15, Agarwal Road, Darya Ganj, New Delhi -110002
Tele: 011- 47630600, 43518550

ॐ **ISBN :** 978-93-25519-29-9

ॐ **PRICE :** ₹100.00

ॐ **PO No :** TXT-XX-XXXXXXX-X-XX


For further information about the books log on to
www.bloomcap.org

Follow us on   

# Preface

*"Future belongs to those Who prepares for it today"*

School Olympiads are National & International level competitions conducted by different Government, Non-Government & Educational Organisations with the purpose of making the children ready to face competitive exams.

The challenging Questions asked in Olympiads motivate them to learn more & more and bring out the best results with improved academic performance. The Awards & Scholarship offered by Olympiads motivate children to aspire & strive for doing better and emerge out to be the best.

## English Olympiads

English is one of the most widely spoken languages across the world. In today's era, good command over English is considered as a must have skill. The greatest advantage of studying English is improvement in communication skills along with the growth of personality.

English Olympiads are meant to strengthen students' command over this universal language by improving spellings, grammar, sentence structure and to master student's language skills.

**'Bloom English Olympiad Study Book Class 10'** is a perfect resource to Study & Practice for Olympiad Exams and other National & State Level Talent Search Exams & Other Competitions.

### Some Special Features of Bloom English Olympiad Study Books are;

- Complete coverage of all the aspects of English; Grammar, Reading Comprehension, Writing Skills, Spellings, Vocabulary & Communication Skills.
- Chapterwise Exercises having different types of Objective Questions at par with the Olympiad Level.
- Olympiad Pattern Practice Sets at the end.

This book is prepared by Expert Panel with the utmost care, still if you have any suggestions regarding its improvement then feel free to contact us at olympiads@bloomcap.org. We will try to inculcate your suggestions in the further editions.

# Contents

# Chapter 01

# Parts of Speech

## 1 Mark Questions

**Directions** (Q. Nos. 1-6) Choose the noun from the following.

1. (a) Trivial       (b) Tormented
   (c) Tremor       (d) Factionalize

2. (a) Albeit       (b) Turncoat
   (c) Overseas     (d) Robust

3. (a) Allocate     (b) Orchestrate
   (c) Bewitching   (d) Dichotomy

4. (a) Anticipate   (b) Accost
   (c) Aggression   (d) Beseech

5. (a) Promulgate   (b) Inaugurate
   (c) Historic     (d) Transmission

6. (a) Jargon       (b) Ensuing
   (c) Obnoxious    (d) Abominable

**Directions** (Q. Nos. 7-12) Choose the correct pronoun to fill the blanks.

7. Can you help ......... please?
   (a) mine       (b) me
   (c) my         (d) I

8. Aman: Somebody called while you were at lunch.
   Nita: Oh! Did ...... leave a message?
   (a) it
   (b) he
   (c) she
   (d) they

9. Is that car ...... ?
   (a) our        (b) yours
   (c) their      (d) him

10. ...... newspaper do you read—The Hindu or The Times of India?
    (a) What       (b) Which
    (c) Whose      (d) Who

11. Make sure ....... school supplies are ready for the next day.
    (a) you're     (b) your
    (c) ours       (d) hers

12. The children cleaned their room all by ........... .
    (a) themselves (b) itself
    (c) himself    (d) hisself

**Directions** (Q. Nos. 13-17) Use suitable modals to fill the blanks.

13. Passengers ...... to talk to the driver while the bus is in motion.
    (a) will not
    (b) ought not
    (c) shall not
    (d) do not

14. We've run out of paper clips. I ...... get some more in the evening.
    (a) should     (b) need
    (c) must       (d) may

**15.** Promila ...... have told her brother about this deal as it was supposed to be absolutely confidential.

    (a) mustn't        (b) needn't

    (c) shouldn't     (d) doesn't

**16.** Shall we go skating or stay at home? Which ...... do yourself?

    (a) should you rather

    (b) would you rather

    (c) will you rather

    (d) do you rather

**17.** Cases of Covid positive patients ...... be reported to the authorities.

    (a) may          (b) can

    (c) should      (d) must

**Directions** (Q. Nos. 18-22) Choose the correct meaning of the underlined modals in the following sentences.

**18.** You <u>can't</u> wear jeans at work.

    (a) Impossibility   (b) Probability

    (c) Prohibition    (d) Obligation

**19.** Did you know that Federer <u>could</u> play tennis when he was eight?

    (a) Ability       (b) Possibility

    (c) Permission    (d) Probability

**20.** I know you're very busy, but <u>might</u> I ask you a quick question.

    (a) Ability       (b) Permission

    (c) Certainty    (d) Prohibition

**21.** You <u>must</u> make sure that you bring all the required documents.

    (a) Permission   (b) Certainty

    (c) Possibility    (d) Obligation

**22.** You <u>must</u> be really happy when you got Rank 1 in the JEE Entrance Test.

    (a) Probability   (b) Ability

    (c) Certainty    (d) Willingness

**Directions** (Q. Nos. 23-26) Choose the verbs from the words listed in the options.

**23.** (a) Placid       (b) Unruly

    (c) Underline    (d) Raptor

**24.** (a) Placate     (b) Tired

    (c) Rather      (d) Commotion

**25.** (a) Recess      (b) Envelope

    (c) Pictorial     (d) Envelop

**26.** (a) Humane     (b) Stalk

    (c) Overseas    (d) Tranquil

**Directions** (Q. Nos. 27-31) Fill in the blanks by choosing the correct word from the options.

**27.** The criminal had managed to ......... several times, but was finally ...... by the police.

    (a) deceive, cheated

    (b) defend, acquitted

    (c) escape, arrested

    (d) cheat, robbed

**28.** I would like to ...... your attention to the last paragraph of my letter ...... to the terms of the sale of the goods.

    (a) invite, according

    (b) Withdraw, regarding

    (c) react, mainly

    (d) draw, pertaining

**29.** The secretary ...... the society's funds, so he was ....... .

    (a) misplaced, charge

    (b) rolled, challaned

    (c) pirated, dismissed

    (d) misappropriated, dismissed

**30.** The spirit or alcohol that a doctor ...... on our arm before .......... an injection is an example of an antiseptic.

    (a) rubs, giving     (b) rubbed, giving

    (c) dabs, piercing   (d) puts, forcing

**31.** The attempt of the robbers was ...... because the travellers ...... enough fortitude.
 (a) encouraged, described
 (b) foiled, showed
 (c) failed, showed
 (d) encountered, had

**Directions** (Q. Nos. 32-37) Complete the blanks with suitable articles.

**32.** When I was born, I was so surpised that I couldn't talk for ...... year and ...... half. (Grace Allen)
 (a) a, a  (b) a, an
 (c) a, the  (d) the, the

**33.** ...... dog is ...... only thing on earth that loves you more than you love yourself. (Josh Billings)
 (a) The, the  (b) A, the
 (c) A, a  (d) An, a

**34.** Amercians like fat books and ...... thin women. (Russell Baker)
 (a) an  (b) the
 (c) a  (d) No article

**35.** ...... death is ...... nature's way of telling you to slow down. (Anonymous)
 (a) An, the
 (b) The, a
 (c) A, a
 (d) No article, No article

**36.** When I was ...... boy of fourteen, my father was so ignorant I could hardly stand to have ...... old man around. But when I got to be twenty - one, I was astonished at how much he had learned in seven years. (Mark Twain)
 (a) a, a
 (b) a, an
 (c) a, the
 (d) a, No article

**37.** ...... banker is ...... man who lends you ...... umbrella when ...... weather is fair, and takes it away from you when it rains. (Anonymous)
 (a) A, a, an, a
 (b) A, a, an, the
 (c) A, the, an, the
 (d) The, a, an, the

**Directions** (Q. Nos. 38-40) Select the adjectives used in the following sentences.

**38.** I saw a really good show on TV last night.
 (a) really  (b) good
 (c) last  (d) Both (b) and (c)

**39.** That Dracula film was absolutely terrifying.
 (a) film  (b) absolutely
 (c) terrifying  (d) was

**40.** We were really bored as we had nothing to do during the weekend curfew.
 (a) really
 (b) nothing
 (c) weekend
 (d) bored and weekend

**Directions** (Q. Nos. 41 and 42) Choose the sentences with the correct order of adjectives in them.

**41.** (a) Drishti spotted a handsome young man standing outside the iron black gate.
 (b) Drishti spotted a young handsome man standing outside the black iron gate.
 (c) Dristi spotted a handsome young man standing outside the iron gate black.
 (d) Drishti spotted a handsome young man standing outside the black iron gate.

**42.** (a) The silly young woman dropped the tasty Chinese food on her comfortable new bed.

   (b) The silly young woman dropped the tasty Chinese food on her new comfortable bed.

   (c) The young silly woman dropped the Chinese tasty food on her new comfortable bed.

   (d) The young silly woman dropped the tasty food Chinese on her new comfortable bed.

**Directions** (Q. Nos. 43-47) Use appropriate adverbs to fill the blanks in the following sentences.

**43.** As he had not prepared his lessons well, he walked ...... towards his teacher.

   (a) confidently     (b) hesitantly

   (c) glowingly     (d) abruptly

**44.** Your English is ...... getting better.

   (a) alarmingly

   (b) may be

   (c) definitely

   (d) sequentially

**45.** Pallavi was ...... frowning at the suggestion but was soon advocating it herself.

   (a) initially     (b) finally

   (c) majorly     (d) lastingly

**46.** Whenever things go ........ at home, my younger sister, Japjot, gets blamed.

   (a) alright     (b) well

   (c) quietly     (d) wrong

**47.** Nitin is ...... calm but today he appears ........ disturbed.

   (a) rarely, rather

   (b) usually, rather

   (c) highly, rather

   (d) quietly, almost

**Directions** (Q. Nos. 48-51) Choose the sentence with the correct use of conjunctions.

**48.** (a) We wanted to go to the show so there weren't any seats left.

   (b) We wanted to go to the show as there weren't any seats left.

   (c) We wanted to go to the show but there weren't any seats left.

   (d) We wanted to go to the show because there weren't any seats left.

**49.** (a) We know he has funny dreams and he laughs in his sleep.

   (b) We know he has funny dreams because he laughs in his sleep.

   (c) We know he has funny dreams but he laughs in his sleep.

   (d) We know he has funny dreams although he laughs in his sleep.

**50.** (a) Burgers are very tasty because they are not very healthy.

   (b) Burgers are very tasty and they are not very healthy.

   (c) Burgers are very tasty so they are not very healthy.

   (d) Burgers are very tasty although they are not very healthy.

**51.** (a) Pick me up early, please, so we don't get late.

   (b) Pick me up early, please, and we don't get late.

   (c) Pick me up early, please, although we don't get late.

   (d) Pick me up early, please, or we don't get late.

**Directions** (Q. Nos. 52-56) Choose appropriate word from the options to fill the blanks.

**52.** Weather conditions have improved ....... the last few days.

   (a) by     (b) throughout

   (c) over     (d) until

**53.** The train is supposed ...... arrive ...... New Delhi Station in a few minutes.

   (a) to, in   (b) at, at   (c) by, at   (d) to, at

**54.** Akshay was stabbed ...... the back while he was going ...... a drink.
(a) at, for
(b) in, to
(c) in, for
(d) into, from

**55.** Take some extra money ...... you. It'll come ...... handy.

(a) with, in
(b) for, on
(c) to, for
(d) by, on

**56.** There is a small table ...... the bed ...... which my papers are kept.
(a) besides, at
(b) beside, on
(c) next, on
(d) in, on

## 2 Marks Questions

**57.** Which of the following statements is/are TRUE?
A. 'The' is a definite article.
B. 'Blunder' is a countable noun.
C. 'Unkempt' is an adverb.
C. 'Sparingly' is an adjective.
**Codes**
(a) A and C
(b) B and C
(c) A and D
(d) A and B

**58.** Match the words given in List I with the parts of speech given in List II.

| List I | | List II | |
| --- | --- | --- | --- |
| A. | Panorama | 1. | Preposition |
| B. | Figurative | 2. | Verb |
| C. | Scavenge | 3. | Adjective |
| D. | Towards | 4. | Noun |

**Codes**

| | A | B | C | D | | A | B | C | D |
| --- | --- | --- | --- | --- | --- | --- | --- | --- | --- |
| (a) | 4 | 3 | 1 | 2 | (b) | 4 | 3 | 2 | 1 |
| (c) | 2 | 1 | 3 | 4 | (d) | 1 | 3 | 2 | 4 |

**59.** Choose the sentence(s) that is/are grammatically correct and meaningful.
A. It was a mistake on my part to have invited Naresh to dinner.
B. Why don't you ask him to leave your place?
C. There will be no regular garbages collection due to the ongoing pandemic.
D. The PM reached the venue latter than expected.

**Codes**
(a) A and B
(b) C and D
(c) Only A
(d) Only D

**60.** Read the following statement and choose the correct option.
A. 'The' is used before 'Netherlands'.
B. 'Recycle' is a verb while 'Recycled' is an adjective.
C. 'Pester' is a verb while 'Lockdown' is a noun.
D. 'Barbaric' is an adverb.
(a) TTTT (b) TTFF (c) TTTF (d) TFTF

**Directions** (Q. Nos. 61-64) Choose the part of the sentence that has an error. In case there is no error, mark option (d) i.e. 'No Error' as your answer.

**61.** (A) Nishtha closely (B) resembles with his father in (C) facial features.
(a) A
(b) B
(c) C
(d) No error

**62.** (A) Don't stop anywhere, (B) go home (C) fastly.
(a) A    (b) B    (c) C    (d) No error

**63.** (A) The faster (B) you drive, (C) the most dangerous it is.
(a) A
(b) B
(c) C
(d) No error

**64.** (A) Order has been issued (B) for his transfer (C) to another state.
(a) A    (b) B    (c) C    (d) No error

# Chapter 02

# Subject-Verb Agreement

## 1 Mark Questions

**Directions** (Q. Nos. 1-6) Choose the correct option to complete the sentence.

1. Climbing up steep mountain slopes ......... both endurance and stamina.
   (a) require
   (b) requires
   (c) required
   (d) requiring

2. After using the computer for a long time, looking into the distance for about five minutes ...... the eyes.
   (a) relax
   (b) relaxes
   (c) relaxed
   (d) relaxing

3. The disabled ...... easier access to public buildings.
   (a) demand
   (b) has demanding
   (c) were demanded
   (d) demanding

4. The French ...... noted for their food and fashion.
   (a) are
   (b) is
   (c) was
   (d) has

5. Buying a life insurance policy ...... to ensure your children have some security.
   (a) help
   (b) helps
   (c) helped
   (d) helping

6. At least half an hour of exercise a day ......... wonders for one's health.
   (a) do
   (b) does
   (c) done
   (d) doing

**Directions** (Q. Nos. 7-9) Which of the following sentences given in the options have the correct usage of Subject-Verb Agreement.

7. (a) Two hours is a long time to wait for a taxi or a bus.
   (b) Nothing have been determined as of yet.
   (c) The elderly has special seats set aside for them in the DTC buses.
   (d) The causes of this prevalent disease is bad diet and lack of exercise.

8. (a) The poor in every countries deserves to have access to education.
   (b) Namita is wearing a black and white saree.
   (c) The first and the fifth chapter of this book is very difficult.
   (d) A year and a half are wasted.

9. (a) A pair of spectacles have been bought by me.
   (b) Orders for Ramesh's transfer has been issued.
   (c) Politics is a dirty game.
   (d) Two series of matches was played last year.

**Directions** (Q. Nos. 10-14) Choose the part of the sentence that has an error. In case there is no error, mark option (d) i.e. 'No error' as your answer.

**10.** Due to the snow the marks was unrecognisable.
(a) Due to the
(b) snow the
(c) marks was unrecognisable
(d) No error

**11.** The promoters of Medcity Hospitals has agreed to sell their business to Primus Hospitals.
(a) The promoters of
(b) Medcity Hospitals has agreed
(c) to sell their business to Primus Hospitals
(d) No error

**12.** The commander of the ship as well as the crew are caught in the storm.
(a) The commander of
(b) the ship as well as the crew
(c) are caught in the storm
(d) No error

**13.** It is easy to fall victim not only to those who may hurt or mistreats us, but also to our own anger.
(a) It is easy to fall victim
(b) not only to those who may hurt or mistreats us,
(c) but also to our own anger
(d) No error

**14.** Measles has broken out in the town.
(a) Measles has      (b) broken out
(c) in the town      (d) No error

## 2 Marks Questions

**15.** Choose the sentence(s) in which subject verb agreement is not followed properly.
A. Breaking and entering is against the law.
B. A car and a bike are parked in front of my house.
C. Neither the cups nor the saucer is kept on the table.
D. Each of these items are found in South America.
**Codes**
(a) A, B and C      (b) A and B
(c) Only D      (d) Only C

**Directions** (Q. Nos. 16-20) Given below is a sentence that contains a subject verb agreement error. Choose the option with no such error.

**16.** Our dog Cinderella, together with her seven puppies, have chewed all the stuffing out of the sofa cushions.
A. Our dog Cinderella, together with her seven puppies, have chews all the stuffing out of the sofa cusions.
B. Our dog Cinderella, together with her seven puppies, has chewed all the stuffing out of the sofa cushions.
C. Our dog Cinderella, together with her seven puppies, had chewed all the stuffing out of thc sofa cushions.
D. Our dog Cinderella, together with her seven puppies, chews all the stuffing out of the sofa cushions.
**Codes**
(a) Only A      (b) B, C and D
(c) B and C      (d) C and D

**17.** Neither of my two elder brothers has invest money wisely.
A. Neither of my two elder brothers invests money wisely.
B. Neither of my two elder brothers invest money wisely.

    C. Neither of my two elder brothers have invested money wisely.

    D. Neither of my two elder brothers invested money wisely.

**Codes**

(a) A and D

(b) B, C and D

(c) A, C and D

(d) A, B and C

18. Although I broken my arm, I still have cheer for the team.

    A. Although I broken my arm, I still had cheer for the team.

    B. Although I break my arm, I still cheered for the team.

    C. Although I broke my arm, I still cheered for the team.

    D. Although I had broken my arm, I still cheered for the team.

**Codes**

(a) C and D      (b) Only C

(c) A and D      (d) B and A

19. Mike is one of those students who never brings a pen to writing class.

    A. Mike is one of those students who never will brought a pen to writing class.

    B. Mike is one of those students who never has brought a pen to writing class.

    C. Mike is one of those students who never bring a pen to writing class.

    D. Mike is one of those students who never brought a pen to writing class.

**Codes**

(a) Only A      (b) Only B

(c) Only C      (d) Only D

20. They always say time changes things, but you actually has to changed them yourself.

    A. They always say time changed things, but you actually have to change them yourself.

    B. They always say time change things, but you actually has to change them yourself.

    C. They always say time changes things, but you actually have to change them yourself.

    D. They always say time change things, but you actually changes them yourself.

**Codes**

(a) Only C      (b) A and C

(c) B and D      (d) B, C and D

21. Choose the sentence(s) in which subject verb agreement is followed properly.

    A. Cattle is grazing in the field.

    B. Mathematics is a difficult subject.

    C. The police was posted all over the route.

    D. Our new premises are located on MG Road.

**Codes**

(a) A and B      (b) B and C

(c) Only D      (d) B and D

# Tenses

## 1 Mark Questions

**Directions** (Q. Nos 1-10) Choose the most suitable alternative in accordance with the correct use of tense.

1. (a) Nishit seldom has fatty food.
   (b) Nishit is seldom having fatty food.
   (c) Nishit has seldom had fatty food.
   (d) Nishit is seldom have fatty food.

2. (a) It is looking that it may rain.
   (b) It is looked that it may rain.
   (c) It looks that it may rain.
   (d) It is being looking that it may rain.

3. (a) Niharika just had her lunch.
   (b) Niharika just have her lunch.
   (c) Niharika has just had her lunch.
   (d) Niharika have just had her lunch.

4. (a) While they were having lunch, lights going out.
   (b) While they were having lunch, lights went out.
   (c) While they had lunch, lights went out.
   (d) While they were having lunch, lights have gone out.

5. (a) In a week's time, I will completed my work.
   (b) In a week's time, I will have completed my work.
   (c) In a week's time, I will be completed my work.
   (d) In a week's time, I will completes my work.

6. (a) Preeti did not open the door because she had washed her hair.
   (b) Preeti did not open the door because she washed her hair.
   (c) Preeti did not opened the door because she washed her hair.
   (d) Preeti did not open the door because she was washing her hair.

7. (a) By five o'clock yesterday, I caught only one fish.
   (b) By five o'clock yesterday, I have caught only one fish.
   (c) By five o'clock yesterday, I has caught only one fish.
   (d) By five o'clock yesterday, I had caught only one fish.

8. (a) After Mukul had rested for a while, he started on his journey.
   (b) After Mukul rested for a while, he started on his journey.
   (c) After Mukul rested for a while, he had started on his journey.
   (d) After Mukul has rested for a while, he started on his journey.

9. (a) Karna lived in London for two years when I went there.
   (b) Karna was living in London for two years when I gone there.
   (c) Karna had been living in London for two years when I went there.
   (d) Karna has been living in London for two years when I went there.

10. (a) Last week Shreya had gone to the cinema twice.
    (b) Last week Shreya went to the cinema twice.
    (c) Last week Shreya have gone to the cinema twice.
    (d) Last week Shreya had going to the cinema twice.

**Directions** (Q. Nos. 11-20) Choose the correct tenses from the options to fill in the blanks.

11. ...... Frank in Toronto?
    (a) Did you meet
    (b) Have you met
    (c) Were you meeting
    (d) Will you met

12. He had a break after he ...... for two hours.
    (a) was walking
    (b) had been walking
    (c) has walked
    (d) walk

13. I ...... her for a long time.
    (a) know
    (b) have known
    (c) have been knowing
    (d) had knew

14. We ...... the windows and the car on Saturday morning.
    (a) was cleaning
    (b) cleaned
    (c) have been cleaning
    (d) will cleaned

15. I ....... in York for a week in 1998.
    (a) worked
    (b) have been working
    (c) have worked
    (d) will be working

16. I ...... you in your office with a girl! Really? We ........ .
    (a) saw, have just talked
    (b) have seen, just talked
    (c) saw, were just talking
    (d) had seen, have been just talking

17. How many cupboards ...... since yesterday?
    (a) did they moved
    (b) have they moved
    (c) have they been moving
    (d) they moved

18. As he ...... a bike, a dog ...... him.
    (a) was riding, bit
    (b) rode, bite
    (c) was riding, has bitten
    (d) had been riding, bit

19. When the dog ...... him, he ...... his bike.
    (a) was biting, fall off
    (b) bit, was falling off
    (c) bit, fell off
    (d) had bit, fell off

20. I can't stand it anymore. I ...... the furniture since breakfast.
    (a) am polishing
    (b) have been polishing
    (c) have polished
    (d) was polishing

# 2 Marks Questions

**21.** Which of the following sentences are in simple present tense?

A. The Earth revolves around the Sun.

B. Do they get up late?

C. Rama has been working in Wipro since July, 2018.

D. Nidhi has applied for admission to Delhi University.

**Codes**

(a) A, B and C     (b) A and D

(c) B and D     (d) A and B

**22.** Identify the given sentences as T (True) and F (False). Choose from the options given below.

A. "Susan will have been ready by the time I get home." The given sentence is in future perfect tense.

B. "I was washing the dishes when the phone rang." The given sentence is in simple past tense.

C. "I have already prepared breakfast." The given sentence is in present perfect tense.

D. "I will call him as soon as possible." The given sentence is in future continuous tense.

(a) TFFF   (b) TFTF   (c) FTFT   (d) TTTT

**23.** Which of the following sentences are in simple past tense?

A. I used to go to school every day.

B. Rachna has been cleaning the cupboard since 3 PM.

C. When did they leave the office?

D. At noon, I had been playing cricket for 3 hours.

**Codes**

(a) A, B and C

(b) A and C

(c) B and C

(d) B, C and D

**24.** Which of these sentences is/are not in future perfect continuous tense?

A. I will not have been shopping on wednesday, you can come to see me.

B. I will have helped him to do the task before the class starts.

C. By the end of this week, will I have been living with him for five months?

D. My mother will not have prepared breakfast by the time my father and brother wake up.

**Codes**

(a) B and D

(b) C and D

(c) A and C

(d) A and B

**Directions** (Q. Nos. 25 and 26) Which of the following sentences have the correct use of tenses?

**25.** A. She is brushing her teeth every night.

B. I know her since 1999.

C. Nutan has written ten e-mails since morning.

D. I don't think we met before.

**Codes**

(a) A and B     (b) Only C

(c) Only D     (d) C and D

**26.** A. When I called on Prisha, she was doing her homework.

B. I have received your letter this morning.

C. Peehu did not cook her breakfast yet.

D. They have been owning this property for the last seven years.

**Codes**

(a) Only C

(b) A and C

(c) Only A

(d) Only D

# Chapter 04

# Clauses and Conditionals

## 1 Mark Questions

**Directions** (Q. Nos. 1-10) Identify the type of clauses in the following sentences.

1. I do not know if Prisha would come.
   (a) Adjective clause
   (b) Noun clause
   (c) Adverb clause
   (d) No clause

2. Rajat knows the boy who came here last night.
   (a) Adverb clause    (b) Noun clause
   (c) Adjective clause (d) No clause

3. Naina is so weak that she cannot run.
   (a) Noun caluse      (b) Adjective clause
   (c) Adverb clause    (d) No clause

4. Everyone knows Nishit has come.
   (a) Noun clause
   (b) Adjective clause
   (c) Adverb clause
   (d) No clause

5. This is the reason why Pankaj has not passed.
   (a) Adjective clause (b) Noun clause
   (c) Adverb clause    (d) No clause

6. Since Nupur is ill, she cannot go out.
   (a) Noun clause      (b) Adverb clause
   (c) Adjective clause (d) No clause

7. I shall do whatever my father says.
   (a) Adjective clause (b) Adverb clause
   (c) Noun clause      (d) No clause

8. We are happy that she is successful.
   (a) Adverb clause    (b) Adjective clause
   (c) Noun clause      (d) No clause

9. I like to go surfing on Saturdays.
   (a) Adverb clause
   (b) Adjective clause
   (c) Noun clause
   (d) No clause

10. I know the house which he got built last year.
    (a) Adjective clause (b) Noun clause
    (c) Adverb clause    (d) No clause

**Directions** (Q. Nos. 11-15) Identify the principal clause in the following sentences.

11. The boy stated that his brother would not leave.
    (a) The boy          (b) that his brother
    (c) The boy stated   (d) would not come

12. The girl who lives here said that her sister would not come.
    (a) The girl who lives here
    (b) The girl said
    (c) her sister would not come
    (d) that her sister would not come

13. You should be content and pleased with what you have these days.
    (a) You should be content
    (b) and pleased with
    (c) You should be content and pleased with
    (d) what you have these days

14. She knows that she would make a mark in life.
    (a) She knows that
    (b) She would make a mark
    (c) mark in life
    (d) She knows

15. Mr Pantal asked his party men to find out if they could help him with this issue.
    (a) Mr Pantal asked
    (b) if they could help him with this issue
    (c) asked his party men
    (d) Mr Pantal asked his party men to find out

## 2 Marks Questions

**Directions** (Q. Nos. 16-25) Fill in the blanks by choosing the correct option.

16. If I …… rich, I would buy a BMW.
    (a) was          (b) am
    (c) were         (d) are

17. If I drink cola, I …… a burning sensation in my stomach.
    (a) got          (b) will get
    (c) had got      (d) would get

18. If I had known Mintoo was unwell, I …… helped him.
    (a) had          (b) would had
    (c) will         (d) would have

19. If the weather is fine, we …… go out for picnic.
    (a) should       (b) have
    (c) will         (d) would have

20. If Tanya …… money, she could have enjoyed the picnic.
    (a) had brought   (b) had bought
    (c) have brought  (d) brought

21. In case you don't make noise, you …… live here.
    (a) should       (b) can
    (c) will         (d) would

22. If Nupur ……… intelligent, she would not do it.
    (a) was          (b) if
    (c) had          (d) were

23. If you …… so long to dress up, we would have reached the venue by now.
    (a) had taken    (b) hadn't taken
    (c) have taken   (d) have took

24. Naira would go to the hospital if she …… to get vaccinated.
    (a) had wanted   (b) wanted
    (c) will want    (d) wants

25. If I … clean my room, my mother …… make pasta for me.
    (a) am, will
    (b) don't, won't
    (c) won't, doesn't
    (d) am not, isn't

# Collocations

## 1 Mark Questions

**Directions** (Q. Nos. 1-5) Choose the sentences which do not collocate properly.

1. (a) He gave me a piece of advice.
   (b) Sushil came up with an idea to solve the problem.
   (c) Gyan looks after his siblings when his parents are not around.
   (d) This problem is highly easy.

2. (a) Sushma packed her bags and left for her hometown when lockdown was announced.
   (b) Could you please make a cup of coffee for me?
   (c) I swiftly agree to the idea you proposed.
   (d) The Covid-19 virus causes a deadly disease.

3. (a) I think you must take a break now.
   (b) Nisha just can't leave up smoking.
   (c) The crowds cheered up the home team.
   (d) Would you like to open an account at our bank?

4. (a) He burst into laughter when he saw his father dressed as a clown.
   (b) We had a brief discussion today.
   (c) There is a sharp turn at the end of this road.
   (d) Give me a favour, please.

5. (a) It was greatly cold today morning.
   (b) A large population of Delhi is infected with Covid-19.
   (c) Neha took the charge of Vice Principal today.
   (d) There is a steep rise in the price of petrol this year.

**Directions** (Q. Nos. 6-15) Fill in the blanks with the most appropriate option.

6. The ........ killer was finally nabbed by the police.
   (a) stately (b) serial (c) cereal (d) clever

7. She ...... confident of winning the elections.
   (a) sounded      (b) rounded
   (c) spoke      (d) funded

8. The Corona ...... has hit the entire world.
   (a) onset      (b) outbreak
   (c) outage      (d) hostage

9. Sachin was given a ...... ovation when he appeared in his 100th Test match.
   (a) steady      (b) landing
   (c) standing      (d) handy

10. The PM was ...... aware of the economic status of our country.
   (a) folly      (b) steeply
   (c) fully      (d) bluntly

**11.** The …… finale of the competition was held in Brisbane.
(a) great
(b) grind
(c) last
(d) grand

**12.** Did you take the job …… survey?
(a) setting
(b) satisfaction
(c) sequencing
(d) alert

**13.** One must …… to the expectations of one's teachers and parents.
(a) live on
(b) seek up
(c) live up
(d) stay up

**14.** Which of the following does not collocate with 'have'?
(a) lunch
(b) a shower
(c) courage
(d) music

**15.** Which of the following does not collocate with 'make'?
(a) amends
(b) noise
(c) homage
(d) plans

**Directions** (Q. Nos. 16-20) Choose the sentences which are collocated properly.

**16.** (a) India has a straight chance of winning the World Cup.
(b) Why don't you improve your soft skills?
(c) The poor couldn't afford even a single rectangle meal during the lockdown.
(d) The company priority does not mention anything about sick leaves.

**17.** (a) The company launched a massive advertising campaign to launch their new product.
(b) Ritesh was viewing TV when I called him.
(c) I take to gym every morning.
(d) Sushmita took a presentation in no time.

**18.** (a) Pragya was quickly disappointed when her name did not appear in the merit list.
(b) I was filled with horror when I heard about the brutal murder of my neighbours.
(c) The PM was given a hot welcome in Bangladesh.
(d) The actress cheated the show as the lead star in the movie.

**19.** (a) There is no need to get offence as it was just a prank.
(b) The football match had to be postponed due to lighter rains.
(c) He wanted to strike up a business so he took a loan.
(d) Karishma turned up late for the office today.

**20.** (a) The traffic police started a campaign to creak down on speeding drivers.
(b) Pranutan looked upon the meaning of the word in the dictionary.
(c) The youngsters keep up with the latest fashions.
(d) Mother Teresa always shook pity on the dying destitutes.

## 2 Marks Questions

**21.** Match the words in List I with those given in List II to make appropriate collocations.

| List I | | List II | |
|---|---|---|---|
| A. | Pitch | 1. | Contagious |
| B. | Sharp | 2. | Dark |
| C. | Utter | 3. | Contrast |
| D. | Highly | 4. | Disaster |

**Codes**

| | A | B | C | D | | A | B | C | D |
|---|---|---|---|---|---|---|---|---|---|
| (a) | 2 | 3 | 1 | 4 | (b) | 4 | 1 | 2 | 3 |
| (c) | 3 | 2 | 1 | 4 | (d) | 2 | 3 | 4 | 1 |

**22.** Which of the following sentences use collocations properly?
A. He had a fatal accident yesterday.
B. Many youngsters are brand conscious these days.

C. Did you hear about the golden scheme?

D. He heaped a sigh of relief on seeing his missing parents.

**Codes**

(a) A, B and C　　(b) C and D
(c) A and B　　　(d) Only B

23. With reference to collocations, which of these statements is/are wrong?

    A. The word 'dismount' is used with 'cyclists'.

    B. 'Crashing bore' is a collocation.

    C. 'Make' does not collocate with 'bed'.

    D. 'Social' does not go with 'distancing'.

    **Codes**

    (a) A and B　　　(b) C and D
    (c) B, C and D　　(d) A and C

24. Which of the following labelled words collocate with each other?

    A: Human　　　B: Fitting
    C: Hour　　　　D: Shoulder
    E: Cold　　　　F: Reply
    G: Error　　　　H: Earth
    I: Care　　　　J: Storage

    (a) A - G and B - E
    (b) A - G, E - D and D - F
    (c) A - G, B - F and E - J
    (d) B - F, E - J and H - I

25. With reference to collocations, identify the given sentences as T (True) and F (False). Choose from the options given below.

    A. 'Take a mistake' is an appropriate collocation.

    B. 'Rush hour' and 'Junk food are appropriate' collocations.

    C. 'Strongly' and 'opposed' do not go with each other.

    D. 'Biting' and 'remark' do not collocate with each other.

    (a) FTFF　　　　(b) FTFT
    (c) FFFF　　　　(d) TTTT

26. Which of the following sentences do not use collocations properly?

    A. My father had a massive heart attack on June 5th.

    B. The doctor asked him to take rewarding exercise.

    C. The Titanic sank on its maiden voyage.

    D. We don't have heavy evidence that they have used drugs.

    **Codes**

    (a) A and C　　　(b) B, C and D
    (c) Only D　　　(d) B and D

27. Match the words in List I with these given in List II to make suitable collocations.

| List I | | List II | |
|---|---|---|---|
| A. | Make | 1. | Your emotions |
| B. | Get over | 2. | Packet |
| C. | Bottle up | 3. | A disappointment |
| D. | Pay | 4. | Steady progress |

**Codes**

|  | A | B | C | D |  |  | A | B | C | D |
|---|---|---|---|---|---|---|---|---|---|---|
| (a) | 4 | 3 | 2 | 1 | | (b) | 2 | 3 | 1 | 4 |
| (c) | 4 | 3 | 1 | 2 | | (d) | 1 | 3 | 2 | 4 |

# Active & Passive Voice

## 1 Mark Questions

**Directions** (Q. Nos. 1-8) Select the correct passive form of the given sentences.

1. The gardener has mowed the lawn.
   (a) The gardener has been mowed by the lawn.
   (b) The lawn has been mowed by the gardener.
   (c) The lawn was mowed by the gardener.
   (d) The lawn is mowed by the gardener.

2. The workers are building the house .
   (a) The house was being built by the workers.
   (b) The house was built by the workers.
   (c) The house is built by the workers.
   (d) The house is being built by the workcrs.

3. Some girls were helping the wounded men.
   (a) The wounded men were helping some girls.
   (b) The wounded men were being helped by some girls.
   (c) The wounded men are being helped by some girls.
   (d) The wounded men received help from some girls.

4. She will finish the thesis in a fortnight.
   (a) The thesis would be finished in a fortnight by her.
   (b) The thesis will finished by her in a fortnight.
   (c) The thesis will be finished by her in a fortnight.
   (d) A fortnight is required to finish the thesis.

5. The cyclone has damaged several crops.
   (a) Several crops had been damaged by the cyclone.
   (b) Several crops are being damaged by the cyclone.
   (c) Several crops have damaged the cyclone.
   (d) Several crops have been damaged by the cyclone.

6. Everyone should obey traffic regulations.
   (a) Traffic regulations should be obeyed by everyone.
   (b) Traffic regulations should be obey by everyone.
   (c) Traffic regulations are obeyed by everyone.
   (d) Traffic regulations will be obeyed by everyone.

7. Bill Gates has given away twenty seven percent of his wealth in charity.
   (a) Twenty seven percent of his wealth had been given away by Bill Gates in charity.
   (b) Twenty seven percent of his wealth has given away Bill Gates in charity.
   (c) Bill Gates has been given away by twenty seven percent of his wealth in charity.
   (d) Twenty seven percent of his wealth has been given away by Bill Gates in charity.

8. The seawater eventually corroded the pillars of the bridge.
   (a) Eventually the pillars of the bridge are being corroded by the seawater.
   (b) Eventually the pillars of the bridge have been corroded by the seawater.
   (c) The pillars of the bridge were eventually corroded by the seawater.
   (d) The pillars of the bridge have been eventually corroded by the seawater.

**Directions** (Q. Nos. 9-13) Choose the correct active form of the given sentences.

9. Good stories are written by Kritika.
   (a) Kritika wrote good stories.
   (b) Kritika has written good stories.
   (c) Kritika writes good stories.
   (d) Kritika is writing good stories.

10. Shreya was called by me last night.
    (a) I called Shreya last night.
    (b) I have called Shreya last night.
    (c) I call Shreya tonight.
    (d) I had called Shreya last night.

11. The work will be finished by 5 PM.
    (a) Someone will finished the work by 5 PM.
    (b) Someone will finish the work by 5 PM.
    (c) Someone has finished the work by 5 PM.
    (d) Someone had finished the work by 5 PM.

12. By what are you made angry?
    (a) What made you angry?
    (b) What is making you angry?
    (c) What will make you angry?
    (d) What makes you angry?

13. You are ordered not to stay here.
    (a) Don't stay here.
    (b) Don't keep staying here.
    (c) Don't stay.
    (d) Get out from here.

**Directions** (Q. Nos. 14-21) Fill in the blanks with active or passive form of verbs by selecting from the given options.

14. The Amazon rainforest is extremely important to the ecology of the Earth. 40% of the world's oxygen ............ (produce) there.
    (a) is produced
    (b) is being produced
    (c) will be produced
    (d) was produced

15. The game ............ (win) by the other team tomorrow. They are a lot better than we are.
    (a) is won          (b) has been won
    (c) will be won     (d) is being won

16. There was a terrible accident on a busy downtown street yesterday. Dozens of people saw it, including my friend, who ............ (interview) by the police.
    (a) has been interviewed
    (b) was interviewed
    (c) will be interviewed
    (d) is being interviewed

**17.** Right now Susan is in the hospital. She ............ (treat) for a bad burn on her hand and arm.

(a) has been treated
(b) was treated
(c) is being treated
(d) is treated

**18.** Yesterday, a bank robber ............ (caught) by the police.

(a) is being caught  (b) was being caught
(c) has been caught (d) was caught

**19.** The painting that ............ by Picasso ............ worthy of exhibition in the art gallery.

(a) is being made, is considered
(b) would have been made, will be considered
(c) was made, are considered
(d) was made, was considered

**20.** All the songs on this new album ............ by Tanya herself and the album ............ live during her recent successful concert tour.

(a) is being written, is being recorded
(b) written, recorded
(c) were written, was recorded
(d) was written, was recorded

**21.** It ............ that the victim ............ with poison.

(a) was thought, had been killed
(b) is thought, has killed
(c) is thought, had been killed
(d) was thought, must have being killed

# 2 Marks Questions

**22.** Which of the following sentences are in Active voice?

A. Be prepared for war.
B. I found Naman's friends laughing at him.
C. My sister, Priyanka, has to buy a new car.
D. The poor should not be looked down upon.

**Codes**

(a) A and B     (b) B and C
(c) C and D     (d) A, B and C

**23.** Choose the option(s) that correctly change(s) the voice of the given sentence.
My best friend showed me some lovely cats in the garden.

A. Some lovely cats in the garden were shown to me by my best friend.
B. I was shown some lovely cats in the garden by my best friend.
C. Some lovely cats in the garden were shown by my best friend.
D. My best friend showed some lovely cats in the garden to me.

**Codes**

(a) Only A
(b) Only C
(c) Both A and B
(d) Both C and D

**24.** Which of the following sentences are in passive voice?

A. The dog was taken for a walk by Shilpa.
B. It is necessary to help the poor.
C. Let a book be brought.
D. I would like someone to help me.

**Codes**

(a) A and B
(b) B and C
(c) A and D
(d) A and C

**25.** Choose the option(s) that correctly change(s) the voice of the given sentence.

Her father had been given an expensive watch by Kavita.

A. Her father had given an expensive watch to Kavita.

B. Kavita had given her father an expensive watch.

C. Kavita had given an expensive watch to her father.

D. Her father was given an expensive watch by Kavita.

**Codes**

(a) Only D          (b) Both B and C

(c) Both A and D    (d) None of these

**26.** Complete the conversation using passive voice by selecting from the given options.

(Natasha has just arrived home from work. Nitin is already there.)

Natasha    Hi! I'm back. Sorry I'm late.

Nitin      Hello. What made you late?

Natasha    I had to use the ring road and I (i)............ (stick) in a traffic jam for forty minutes.

Nitin      Why did you not use the usual route?

Natasha    Because the road (ii) ............ (close) until work on the access road to the new hospital (iii) ........(complete).

(i)  (a) got stuck
     (b) was being stuck
     (c) had been stuck
     (d) stucked

(ii) (a) was closed
     (b) have been closed
     (c) has been closed
     (d) was going to be closed

(iii) (a) was complete
      (b) was going to be completed
      (c) has been completed
      (d) have been completed

# Direct and Indirect Speech

## 1 Mark Questions

**Directions** (Q. Nos. 1-4) Select the correct indirect speech of the given sentences.

1. Nupur says, "I go for a walk every morning".
   (a) Nupur says that she goes for a walk every morning.
   (b) Nupur said that she goes for a walk every morning.
   (c) Nupur says that I go for a walk every morning.
   (d) Nupur said that she went for a walk every morning.

2. I asked the shopkeeper, "What is the price of this bike?"
   (a) I asked the shopkeeper that what the price of this bike was.
   (b) I asked the shopkeeper what is the price of this bike.
   (c) I asked the shopkeeper what was the price of that bike.
   (d) I asked the shopkeeper what the price of that bike was.

3. The coach said, "Don't move, girls".
   (a) The coach told the girls don't move.
   (b) The coach asked the girls not to be moving.
   (c) The coach asked the girls not to move.
   (d) The coach told to them, don't move girls.

4. "Alas! I have broken my father's watch", said Amit.
   (a) Amit was sorrowful that he broke his father's watch.
   (b) Amit exclaimed sorrowfully that he had broken his father's watch.
   (c) Amit exclaimed sorrowfully that he has broken his father's watch.
   (d) Amit was sorrowful that he had broken his father's watch.

**Directions** (Q. Nos. 5-8) Change the following sentences into direct speech.

5. Parul ordered Abhay to go away.
   (a) Parul said to Abhay, "You go away."
   (b) Parul said to Abhay, "I want you to go away."
   (c) Parul says to Abhay, "Go away."
   (d) Parul said to Abhay, "Go away."

6. The interviewer asked Navita why she had left that job.
   (a) The interviewer said, "Why did you leave this job?"
   (b) The interviewer asked Navita, "Why did you left this job?"
   (c) The interviewer said to Navita, "Why did you leave this job?"
   (d) The interviewer asked Navita, "Why are you leaving this job?"

**7.** Father told his daughter that he would attend her PTA meeting the next day.

(a) Father asked his daughter, "I will attend your PTA meeting tomorrow."

(b) Father said to his daughter, "I will attend your PTA meeting the next day."

(c) Father said to his daughter, "I may attend you PTA meeting tomorrow."

(d) Father said to his daughter, "I will attend your PTA meeting tomorrow."

**8.** The boss told Manish that he would be happy if he finished that project by evening.

(a) The boss said to Manish, "I will be happy if you finish this project by evening."

(b) The boss says to Manish, "I will be happy if you finish this project by evening."

(c) The boss said, "I wil be happy if you finish this project by evening."

(d) The boss said, "Manish, finish this project by evening."

**Directions** (Q. Nos. 9-11) Using the indirect speech given in the bracket, fill in the blanks to complete the sentences in direct speech.

**9.** "................" Sue asked.
(Sue asked why they didn't want to go with us.)

(a) "Why don't they want to go with us?"

(b) "Why don't they wish to go with us?"

(c) "Why didn't they want to go with us?"

(d) "Why didn't they wish to go with us?"

**10.** "................" Jasmine said to me.
(Jasmine asked me if my father always came home late.)

(a) "Does your father always come home late?"

(b) "Does your father always had come late?"

(c) "Does your father always have come late?"

(d) "Does your father come home late always?"

**11.** Dhruv said to his grandfather. "............"
(Dhruv asked his grandfather if Grandma was going to take more golf lessons.)

(a) "If Grandma is going to take more golf lessons."

(b) "Is Grandma going to take more golf lessons?"

(c) "Is Grandma going to be taking more golf lessons?"

(d) "Is Gradma going to have taken more golf lessons?"

**Directions** (Q. Nos. 12 and 13) Change these thoughts of people mentioned in the brackets into indirect speech. Choose from the options given below.

**12.** "I've found a new way to get to India."
(*Columbus*)

(a) Columbus thought that he had found a new way to get to India.

(b) Columbus said that he have found a new way to get to India.

(c) Columbus said that he had found a new way to got to India.

(d) Columbus thought that he have found a new way to get to India.

**13.** "That boy will never be a scientist."
(*One of Einstein's teachers*)

(a) One of Einstein's teachers thought that he will never be a scientist.

(b) One of Einstein's teachers thought that he would never be a scientist.

(c) One of Einstein's teachers said that he will never be a scientist.

(d) One of Einstein's teachers told that he would never be a scientist.

# 2 Marks Questions

**14.** Identify the sentences in direct speech and choose T (True) and F (False) from the options accordingly.

A. Michael asked Tom, "Are you married?"

B. He said, "I live in the city center."

C. Teacher said to me, I don't understand you.

D. 'Listen to me!' said mother.

(a) TTFT      (b) TTFF

(c) FFTF      (d) TTTT

**15.** Match the words given in List I with their indirect forms given in List II.

| | List I | | List II |
|---|---|---|---|
| A. | Today | 1. | Then |
| B. | Yesterday | 2. | That day |
| C. | These | 3. | The day before |
| D. | Now | 4. | Those |

**Codes**

| | A | B | C | D | | A | B | C | D |
|---|---|---|---|---|---|---|---|---|---|
| (a) | 2 | 3 | 1 | 4 | (b) | 3 | 2 | 1 | 4 |
| (c) | 3 | 1 | 2 | 4 | (d) | 2 | 3 | 4 | 1 |

**16.** Which of the following statements is/are in indirect narration?

(i) The teacher assured that he would pass his driving test.

(ii) My mother said that I had to study harder.

(iii) Jayesh was in a bad mood today.

(iv) He said that he had seen a good film the previous day.

**Codes**

(a) Only (i)      (b) (i), (ii) and (iv)

(c) All of these      (d) None of these

**17.** Which of the following statements is/are in direct speech?

A. The teacher said, "The First World War started in 1914."

B. He said to Sita I have passed the test.

C. I asked him "where he was going".

D. The captain said to the soldiers, "Attack the enemy."

**Codes**

(a) Only A

(b) Only C

(c) A, C and D

(d) A and D

**18.** Choose the option(s) that correctly change(s) the narration of the given sentence.

The hermit said, "May God make the people of this city live here happily!"

A. The hermit wished that God might make the people of this city live here happily.

B. The hermit wished that God might make the people of that city live there happily.

C. The hermit prayed that God might make the people of that city live there happily.

D. The hermit prayed that God might make the people of this city live here happily.

**Codes**

(a) Both B and C

(b) Both A and D

(c) Both A and C

(d) Both B and D

# Jumbled Sentences

## 1 Mark Questions

**Directions** (Q. Nos. 1-8) Rearrange the following parts to make a meaningful sentence.

1. Pablo Picasso
   P : showed his
   Q : a very young age
   R : truly
   S : exceptional talent from
   (a) PRSQ       (b) SRQP
   (c) PRQS       (d) QSPR

2. I came across
   P : written by my
   Q : an old letter
   R : father when
   S : I was cleaning my cupboard
   (a) QPSR  (b) QPRS (c) PQRS (d) SRQP

3. Biswa stayed
   P : place last night
   Q : because
   R : at his uncle's
   S : his scooter broke down
   (a) RPSQ  (b) SQPR  (c) RPQS  (d) SRPQ

4. With global warming
   P : we have to
   Q : to save the environment
   R : do every bit we can
   S : on the rise,
   (a) PQRS       (b) QRSP
   (c) SPQR       (d) SPRQ

5. Pragya went
   P : to the Netherlands
   Q : in her summer
   R : vacation when she
   S : was in class Vth
   (a) PQSR       (b) PQRS
   (c) SQRP       (d) RPSQ

6. Do you
   P : wearing masks
   Q : and maintaining social
   R : think
   S : distancing can reduce the spread of Covid?
   (a) PQRS       (b) RPSQ
   (c) SQPR       (d) RPQS

7. Alas! our team
   P : final test match
   Q : by six
   R : wickets
   S : lost the
   (a) PRSQ       (b) SRQP
   (c) SPQR       (d) QSPR

8. A lot of
   P : in superstitions
   Q : people
   R : still believe
   S : in India
   (a) QSRP       (b) PRSQ
   (c) PQRS       (d) QSPR

**Directions** (Q. Nos. 9-16) Rearrange the following statements to form a meaningful paragraph.

9. How to open an online bank account?

   P : Fund your account.

   Q : Select your account features and enter your personal information.

   R : Receive documents via secure email, sign electronically and submit.

   S : Set up ID verification questions.

   The proper sequence should be

   (a) QSPR       (b) SQPR

   (c) PSQR       (d) QPSR

10. How to make instant coffee?

    P : Place the instant coffee in the mug.

    Q : Fill the remaining 1/4 of the mug with milk or cream, then stir again.

    R : Boil some water in an electric kettle, then wait for the water to stop simmering.

    S : Fill 3/4 of the cup with the boiled water, then stir with a teaspoon until all the instant coffee is dissolved.

    The proper sequence should be

    (a) PQRS   (b) RPSQ  (c) PRSQ  (d) PSRQ

11. P : The trucks were moving slowly, as there had been heavy snowfall in that area and the roads were slippery with ice.

    Q : Fortunately, the driver of the first truck stopped in time.

    R : A convoy of trucks carrying soldiers was coming down the mountain road.

    S : Suddenly, with a crash, a huge tree on the hillside close to the road fell, bringing along with it boulders and mud.

    The proper sequence should be

    (a) PRSQ

    (b) RPSQ

    (c) PSRQ

    (d) RSQP

12. P : The festival is usually inaugurated with cultural performances and sports shows.

    Q : It, therefore, culminates with the three 'men's games': wrestling, archery and horse racing.

    R : Celebrated for centuries, it is seen as a test of courage, strength, horsemanship and marksmanship.

    S : Mongolia celebrated its biggest national festival, Naadam in July this year.

    The proper sequence should be

    (a) PQRS       (b) SPRQ

    (c) SPQR       (d) SRPQ

13. P : Under the new system, a 3.7 kilometre outfall tunnel will carry treated filtered sewage far out to sea.

    Q : From there, it is dumped into nearby streams and creeks.

    R : People living near these creeks have to live with foul smells and in unhygienic conditions.

    S : In Mumbai's century old system, sewage is collected from homes and factories and piped to various small pumping stations.

    The proper sequence should be

    (a) RPSQ   (b) RSQP  (c) SQRP  (d) PQRS

14. P : He discovered a vaccination for smallpox.

    Q : Edward Jenner was an English surgeon.

    R : It is in fact the world's first vaccine.

    S : Jenner coined the word vaccine from the Latin 'vacca' for cow.

    (a) QPSR   (b) QPRS  (c) PQRS  (d) SRQP

15. P : The reader is likely to find himself emotionally drained by the time he reaches the end of the story.

    Q : This is not at all surprising, for the story, set in India, mesmerises with its storyline and the power of its innovative prose.

R : A tale of love and loss, the novel has sold more than six million copies.

S : Arundathi Roy, an Indian national, won the Booker Prize in 1997 for her novel 'The God of Small Things'.

The proper sequence should be

(a) SRQP      (b) SPQR

(c) RSQP      (d) RQSP

**16.** P : Nigeria is a country in West Africa, situated on the Gulf of Guinea between Benin in the West and Cameron in the East.

Q : With its vast land and large population, Nigeria is rightly nicknamed the 'Giant of Africa'.

R : Its other neighbours are Niger and Chad.

S : The seventh most populous country in the world, Nigeria is also Africa's largest economy.

(a) PQRS

(b) SQRP

(c) PRQS

(d) PRSQ

## 2 Marks Questions

**Directions** (Q. Nos. 17-24) In the following questions, each passage consist of six sentences. The first and sixth sentences are marked as $S_1$ and $S_6$ respectively. The middle four sentences in each have been jumbled up. These are labelled as P, Q, R and S. Find out the proper order of the four sentences.

**17.** $S_1$ A man can be physically confined within stone walls.

P But his mind and spirit will still be free.

Q Thus his freedom of actions may be restricted.

R His hopes and aspiration still remain with him.

S Hence, he will be free spiritually if not physically.

$S_6$ No tyranny can intimidate a lover of liberty.

The proper sequence should be

(a) PQRS      (b) SRQP

(c) QPRS      (d) QPSR

**18.** $S_1$ Once upon a time an ant lived on the bank of a river.

P The dove saw the ant struggling in water in a helpless condition.

Q All its efforts to come up failed.

R One day, it suddenly slipped into water.

S A dove lived in the tree on the bank not far from the spot.

$S_6$ She was touched.

The proper sequence should be

(a) RQSP      (b) QRPS

(c) SRPQ      (d) PQRS

**19.** $S_1$ Duryodhana was a wicked prince.

P One day, Bhima made Duryodhana fall from a tree from which Duryodhana was stealing fruits.

Q He did not like that Pandavas should be loved and respected by the people of Hastinapur.

R Duryodhana specially hated Bhima.

S Among the Pandavas, Bhima was extraordinarily strong and powerful.

$S_6$ This enraged Duryodhana so much that he began to think of removing Bhima from his path.

The proper sequence should be

(a) PSQR      (b) QPRS

(c) QSPR      (d) PSRQ

**20.** $S_1$ The future beckons to us.

P In fact, we have hard work ahead.

Q Where do we go and what shall be our endeavour?

R We shall also have to fight and end poverty, ignorance and disease.

S It will be to bring freedom and opportunity to the common man.

$S_6$ There is no resting for anyone of us till we redeem our pledge in full.

The proper sequence should be

(a) PSRQ      (b) QPSR

(c) QSRP      (d) SRPQ

**21.** $S_1$ Religion is not a matter of mere dogmatic conformity.

P It is not merely going through the ritual prescribed to us.

Q It is not a question of ceremonial piety.

R Unless that kind of transformation occurs, you are not an authentically religious man.

S It is the remaking of your own self, the transformation of your nature.

$S_6$ A man of that character is free from fear, free from hatred.

The proper sequence should be

(a) SPRQ      (b) QPSR

(c) PSRQ      (d) SPQR

**22.** $S_1$ I usually sleep quite well in the train, but this time I slept only a little.

P Most people wanted it shut and I wanted it open.

Q As usual, I got angry about the window.

R The quarrel left me completely upset.

S There were too many people and too much huge luggage all around.

$S_6$ It was shut all night as usual.

The proper sequence should be

(a) RSQP      (b) SQPR

(c) SQRP      (d) RSPQ

**23.** $S_1$ Once King Shantanu met a young and beautiful fisher girl.

P He went to the fisherman and asked him for her hand in marriage.

Q The king was extremely sad and returned to his palace.

R He fell in love with the fisher girl.

S The fisherman agreed to it on condition that the son of his daughter should be heir to the throne of Hastinapur.

$S_6$ Devavrata, the king's son, asked him the reason of his sadness.

The proper sequence should be

(a) PQRS      (b) RPSQ

(c) QSPR      (d) PSQR

**24.** $S_1$ Satyajit Ray made several films for children.

P Later, film-makers have followed his lead.

Q Today, other nations are making children's films in a big way.

R This was at a time when no director considered children as a potential audience.

S Ray was, thus, a pioneer in the field.

$S_6$ But today few think of Ray as a maker of children's films.

The proper sequence should be

(a) PSRQ      (b) RSQP

(c) RSPQ      (d) SQRP

# Chapter 09

# Synonyms and Antonyms

## 1 Mark Questions

**Directions** (Q. Nos. 1-5) Select the most appropriate synonym of the given word.

1. Unruly
   - (a) Cooperative
   - (b) Disobedient
   - (c) Complaint
   - (d) Yielding

2. Deprive
   - (a) Bestow
   - (b) Confer
   - (c) Dispossess
   - (d) Endow

3. Vital
   - (a) Trivial
   - (b) Important
   - (c) Insignificant
   - (d) Needless

4. Judicious
   - (a) Hasty
   - (b) Reckless
   - (c) Irrational
   - (d) Wise

5. Clandestine
   - (a) Secret
   - (b) Truthful
   - (c) Frank
   - (d) Upright

**Directions** (Q. Nos. 6-10) Choose the most appropriate antonym of the given word.

6. Eventual
   - (a) Future
   - (b) Last
   - (c) Overall
   - (d) Initial

7. Conclusive
   - (a) Clear
   - (b) Undeniable
   - (c) Unconvincing
   - (d) Decisive

8. Intrepid
   - (a) Cowardly
   - (b) Invisible
   - (c) Insecure
   - (d) Gallant

9. Choke
   - (a) Stifle
   - (b) Carbon
   - (c) Brave
   - (d) Aid

10. Recede
    - (a) Decrease
    - (b) Wane
    - (c) Enhance
    - (d) Applaud

**Directions** (Q. Nos. 11-13) Choose the odd one out from the following.

11. (a) Affluence
    - (b) Poverty
    - (c) Distress
    - (d) Destitution

12. (a) Pleasure
    - (b) Euphoria
    - (c) Bliss
    - (d) Agony

13. (a) Insipid
    - (b) Tasty
    - (c) Dull
    - (d) Tasteless

**Directions** (Q. Nos. 14-18) Choose the synonym of the underlined word in the following sentences.

14. Natasha is a woman of <u>sterling</u> qualities.
    - (a) Interesting
    - (b) Splendid
    - (c) Irritating
    - (d) Exciting

**15.** Mark Antony's <u>eulogy</u> of Caesar is finally recorded by Shakespeare in his play.
(a) Prayer
(b) Honour
(c) Praise
(d) Denunciation

**16.** It is difficult to <u>discern</u> the sample on the slide without adjusting the microscope.
(a) Discard
(b) Arrange
(c) Determine
(d) Debate

**17.** The convict's <u>ingenuous</u> explanation bought tears in every eye.
(a) Candid
(b) Secret
(c) Insincere
(d) Consistent

**18.** It was an <u>astute</u> move to sell the property at that stage.
(a) Shrewd
(b) Unwise
(c) Dishonest
(d) Inexplicable

**Directions** (Q. Nos. 19-23) Choose the antonym of the underlined word in the following sentences.

**19.** Born in the <u>squalid</u> surroundings of the slums, Prisha rose to stardom.
(a) Dirty
(b) Clean
(c) Disorderly
(d) Mean

**20.** The minister was accused of indulging in <u>nepotism</u>.
(a) Impartiality
(b) Hatred
(c) Condemnation
(d) Indifference

**21.** Throughout the evening, Namita looked very <u>doleful</u>.
(a) Aggressive
(b) Cheerful
(c) Tired
(d) Involved

**22.** In facing adverse situations, Rajeev was very <u>stoical</u>.
(a) Tactless
(b) Awkward
(c) Assured
(d) Impatient

**23.** The forwards of Manchester United made <u>sporadic</u> raids into the opponent's territory.
(a) Rare
(b) Frequent
(c) Sharp
(d) Co-ordinated

## 2 Marks Questions

**24.** Match the words given in List I with their synonyms given in List II.

| List I | List II |
| --- | --- |
| A. Feasible | 1. Unfriendly |
| B. Surly | 2. Practical |
| C. Consolidate | 3. Present |
| D. Current | 4. Centralise |

**Codes**

| | A | B | C | D | | A | B | C | D |
| --- | --- | --- | --- | --- | --- | --- | --- | --- | --- |
| (a) | 2 | 1 | 3 | 4 | (b) | 1 | 2 | 3 | 4 |
| (c) | 4 | 3 | 2 | 1 | (d) | 2 | 1 | 4 | 3 |

**25.** Read the following statements and choose the correct option.
A. 'Incumbent' and 'Obligatory' are synonyms.
B. 'Extreme' and 'Temperate' are antonyms.
C. 'Quest' means 'Search'.
D. 'Meddle' and 'Interfere' are antonyms.
(a) A and C
(b) A, B and C
(c) B and D
(d) Only C

**26.** Which of the following statements are incorrect?

    A. 'Recapitulation' means 'Summarising'.

    B. 'Allay' and 'Reduce' are antonyms.

    C. 'Defiance' and 'Resistance' are antonyms.

    D. 'Reproach' is the synonym of 'Reprimand'.

**Codes**

(a) A and B      (b) B and D

(c) B and C      (d) C and D

**27.** Match the words given in List I with their antonyms given in List II.

| | List I | | List II |
|---|---|---|---|
| A. | Fleeting | 1. | Lasting |
| B. | Prudent | 2. | Admonition |
| C. | Accolade | 3. | Unwise |
| D. | Lucrative | 4. | Unprofitable |

**Codes**

| | A | B | C | D | | A | B | C | D |
|---|---|---|---|---|---|---|---|---|---|
| (a) | 1 | 2 | 3 | 4 | (b) | 4 | 1 | 2 | 3 |
| (c) | 1 | 3 | 2 | 4 | (d) | 3 | 2 | 1 | 4 |

**28.** Which of the following statement(s) is/are correct?

    A. 'Wavy' and 'Lax' are synonyms.

    B. 'Camouflage' means 'to expose'.

    C. 'Impede' and 'Advance' are antonyms.

    D. 'Satisfied' is a synonym of 'smug'.

**Codes**

(a) A and B      (b) A, B and C

(c) Only C      (d) C and D

**Directions** (Q. Nos. 29 and 30) In each of these questions, four words are given marked (A), (B), (C) and (D). Two of these words are most nearly the same or opposite in meaning. Identify these two words.

**29.**    A. Propitious      B. Unreasonable

       C. Favourable      D. Clumsy

    (a) A-B    (b) A-D    (c) B-C    (d) A-C

**30.**    A. Stern      B. Poor

       C. Dwindle      D. Increase

    (a) A-B    (b) B-C    (c) C-D    (d) B-D

# One Word Substitutions

## 1 Mark Questions

**Directions** (Q. Nos. 1-5) Choose an appropriate word for the phrases given below.

1. A large impressive house.
   - (a) Shack
   - (b) Cabin
   - (c) Fort
   - (d) Mansion

2. Impossible or extremely difficult to understand.
   - (a) Incompatible
   - (b) Inaudible
   - (c) Incomprehensible
   - (d) Inevitable

3. A group of singers in a church.
   - (a) Band
   - (b) Choir
   - (c) Troupe
   - (d) Host

4. One who eats too much.
   - (a) Overweight
   - (b) Obese
   - (c) Skinny
   - (d) Glutton

5. Able to adapt to many different functions or activities.
   - (a) Expert
   - (b) Deputy
   - (c) Versatile
   - (d) Talented

**Directions** (Q. Nos. 6-10) Select the correct meaning of the following one word substitutions.

6. Inevitable
   - (a) That which cannot be avoided.
   - (b) That which cannot be seen.
   - (c) That which cannot be understood.
   - (d) That which cannot be eaten.

7. Dermatologist
   - (a) One who treats lung diseases.
   - (b) One who treats skin diseases.
   - (c) One who treats heart diseases.
   - (d) One who treats eye diseases.

8. Aborigines
   - (a) One who lives in a city.
   - (b) One who lives outside his native country.
   - (c) One who is the original inhabitant of a country.
   - (d) One who has lived in many countries.

9. Epitaph
   - (a) Advertisement in a newspaper about a person who has died.
   - (b) A place where dead bodies are kept.
   - (c) The science of making watches.
   - (d) Inscription on a grave.

10. Polyglot
    - (a) A person who has a high degree of skill.
    - (b) A person who knows many subjects.
    - (c) A person who knows many languages.
    - (d) A person who works in customer service.

**Directions** (Q. Nos. 11-14) Choose the odd one out from the following.

11. (a) Democracy    (b) Oligarchy
    (c) Geography    (d) Anarchy

12. (a) Den    (b) Hutch
    (c) Kennel    (d) Grange

13. (a) Oncologist    (b) Radiologist
    (c) Orthopedist    (d) Brigadier

14. (a) Panacea
    (b) Bovine
    (c) Avian
    (d) Equesterian

## 2 Marks Questions

15. Match the words given in List I with the things they are related to given in List II.

| List I | List II |
| --- | --- |
| A. Bale | 1. Sound |
| B. Homicide | 2. Profession |
| C. Anchor | 3. Collection |
| D. Cackle | 4. Killing |

**Codes**

|  | A | B | C | D |  |  | A | B | C | D |
| --- | --- | --- | --- | --- | --- | --- | --- | --- | --- | --- |
| (a) | 3 | 2 | 4 | 1 | | (b) | 4 | 1 | 2 | 3 |
| (c) | 3 | 4 | 2 | 1 | | (d) | 2 | 1 | 3 | 4 |

16. Which of the following statement(s) is/are incorrect?

    A. 'Hangar' is related to aircrafts.
    B. 'Extempore' means spoken without preparation.
    C. 'Autonomy' is related to governance.
    D. One who feeds on human flesh is called a chauvinist.

    **Codes**
    (a) A, B and C    (b) C and D
    (c) Only B    (d) Only D

17. Which of the following one words (enclosed in the box) are related to a place or a profession?

| | |
| --- | --- |
| Asylum | Bevy |
| Ascetic | Elegy |
| Compere | Moo |
| Suicide | Dormitory |
| Invigilator | Insolvent |

    (a) Asylum, Compere, Dormitory and Invigilator
    (b) Asylum, Ascetic, Dormitory and Invigilator
    (c) Compere, Dormitory and Invigilator
    (d) Compere and Invigilator

18. Which of the following statement(s) is/are correct?

    A. A 'numismatist' is one who collects stamps.
    B. 'Screech' is the sound made by parrots.
    C. A 'cartographer' is one who makes maps.
    D. A group of cattle or sheep can be called a 'pride'.

    **Codes**
    (a) A and B
    (b) B and C
    (c) C and D
    (d) Only C

19. Which of the following sentences use one word substitutions properly?

    A. There is a shortage of 'portable' water in India.
    B. An 'extrovert' person does not like to mix with others.
    C. Dogs are kept in 'kennels'.
    D. A 'brood' of chicks was resting in a nest on our mango tree.

    **Codes**
    (a) A and B    (b) B, C and D
    (c) A and C    (d) C and D

# Idioms and Phrases

## 1 Mark Questions

**Directions** (Q. Nos. 1-9) Choose the correct meaning of the following idioms.

**1.** Get cold feet
(a) To run for life
(b) To get cold
(c) To be afraid
(d) To become discourteous

**2.** Wash dirty linen in public
(a) To criticise
(b) To make personal quarrels public
(c) To talk dirty things in public
(d) To wash clothes

**3.** Toe the line
(a) Mark the line
(b) Cross the line
(c) Hit on the toe
(d) Follow others

**4.** To fall flat
(a) To fail to compliment
(b) To fall in love with someone
(c) To give bad news
(d) To fail to produce the intended result

**5.** To lose ground
(a) To become less powerful
(b) To become less popular
(c) To lose foundation
(d) To be without a leader

**6.** To bring to light
(a) To reveal
(b) To conceal
(c) To provide luminiscence
(d) To appeal

**7.** To call a spade a spade
(a) To be frank
(b) To be shy
(c) To be rude
(d) To be diplomatic

**8.** To burn the candle at both ends
(a) To spend cautiously
(b) To be stingy
(c) To workhard
(d) To survive with difficulty

**9.** Build castles in the air
(a) Waste time     (b) Daydream
(c) Build houses     (d) Work hard

**Directions** (Q. Nos. 10-17) Choose the meaning of the underlined idioms/phrases from the options.

**10.** Navneet <u>putacross</u> his ideas to the President.
(a) Made available
(b) Effectively conveyed
(c) Strongly expressed
(d) Laid aside

**11.** People were <u>dropping like flies</u> during the Corona pandemic.

(a) Collapsing in large numbers
(b) Getting infected with many diseases
(c) Taking leave in large numbers
(d) Sitting in the shade

**12.** Parents <u>pay through their nose</u> for their children's education.

(a) Take loans
(b) Pay an extremely high price
(c) Pay a small price
(d) Praise their children's teachers

**13.** Regardless of what Nutan's parents said, she wanted <u>to let her hair down</u>.

(a) Work till late
(b) Wash her hair
(c) Comb her hair
(d) Really enjoy

**14.** Pranjal had to <u>pull strings</u> to get her home loan approved by the manager.

(a) Play music
(b) Use personal influence over important people
(c) Use unfair means
(d) Carry on the orders

**15.** I met my old friend, Samarth, after a long time, but he gave me <u>the cold shoulder</u>.

(a) Scolded me    (b) Insulted me
(c) Abused me    (d) Ignored me

**16.** A match between India and Pakistan always proves to be a <u>big draw</u>.

(a) A keen contest
(b) A huge game
(c) A big source of attraction
(d) A game without any result

**17.** The officer was <u>made a scapegoat</u> for the failure of the project.

(a) Freed from all responsibilities
(b) Suspected of causing
(c) Blamed without reason for
(d) Was severely punished for

**Directions** (Q. Nos. 18-21) Fill in the blanks by choosing the correct phrasal verbs from the given options.

**18.** I do not think Naveen will ever ...... the shock of his mother's death.

(a) get by
(b) get off
(c) get over
(d) get through

**19.** We are ...... of time, the report has to be ready by 8 PM tonight.

(a) running out
(b) running over
(c) running with
(d) run out

**20.** The way Pranutan did the project shows that she has ...... many years of practice.

(a) put out
(b) put on
(c) put off
(d) put in

**21.** The firefighters took several hours to ...... the fire in the newly built quarantine centre.

(a) put in    (b) put out
(c) put on    (d) put off

# 2 Marks Questions

**22.** Match the words given in List I to those given in List II to complete the idioms.

| List I | List II |
|---|---|
| A. Stick to | 1. a new leaf |
| B. No axe | 2. one's guns |
| C. A snake in | 3. to grind |
| D. To turn over | 4. the grass |

**Codes**

|  | A | B | C | D |  |  | A | B | C | D |
|---|---|---|---|---|---|---|---|---|---|---|
| (a) | 2 | 3 | 1 | 4 | | (b) | 3 | 2 | 4 | 1 |
| (c) | 4 | 1 | 2 | 3 | | (d) | 2 | 3 | 4 | 1 |

**23.** Identify the given sentences as T (True) and F (False). Choose from the given options.

A. 'Hit the sack' means go to sleep.

B. 'Oily tongue' means very clear with words.

C. 'Run into' is to meet someone by chance.

D. 'Call off' means to cancel.

(a) FFTF      (b) FFTT

(c) TTTT      (d) TTFF

**24.** Match the phrasal verbs given in List I with their correct meanings given in List II.

| List I | List I |
|---|---|
| A. Fill in | 1. to think of an idea/plan |
| B. Pick up | 2. to take care |
| C. Look after | 3. collect someone in a vehicle to take them somewhere |
| D. Come up with | 4. write information in a form |

**Codes**

|  | A | B | C | D |  |  | A | B | C | D |
|---|---|---|---|---|---|---|---|---|---|---|
| (a) | 2 | 3 | 1 | 4 | | (b) | 4 | 3 | 1 | 2 |
| (c) | 4 | 3 | 2 | 1 | | (d) | 3 | 1 | 2 | 4 |

**Directions** (Q. Nos. 25-27) Consider the given idioms and answer the questions that follow.

A. In a pretty pickle   B. Lose one's head   C. At loggerheads    D. Black sheep

**25.** Which two idioms convey the same meaning?

(a) A and B      (b) B and C

(c) C and D      (d) A and C

**26.** Which of the these idioms talk about a failure or embarrassment?

(a) D     (b) B     (c) C     (d) A

**27.** Which of the these idioms talk about senseless behaviour?

(a) A     (b) B     (c) C     (d) D

**28.** Consider the following statements.

1. He got home from the party all <u>in one piece</u>.

2. He never made a will, <u>to the best of my knowledge</u>.

3. His diet <u>went out the window</u> during holidays.

Which of these statements use the underlined idioms correctly?

(a) 1 and 2      (b) 1 and 3

(c) 2 and 3      (d) All of these

**29.** Match the idioms given in List I with their meanings given in List II.

| List I | List II |
|---|---|
| A. A blessing in disguise | 1. Making a bad situation worse |
| B. Costs an arm and a leg | 2. A good thing that intially seemed bad |
| C. Feeling under the weather | 3. To be very expensive |
| D. Adding insult to injury | 4. Net feeling well |

**Codes**

|  | A | B | C | D |  |  | A | B | C | D |
|---|---|---|---|---|---|---|---|---|---|---|
| (a) | 2 | 3 | 4 | 1 | | (b) | 2 | 3 | 1 | 4 |
| (c) | 4 | 1 | 2 | 3 | | (d) | 3 | 2 | 1 | 4 |

# Cloze Test

## 1 Mark Questions

**Directions** (Q. Nos. 1-45) Read the passages given below and fill in the blanks with suitable options.

### Passage I

Big Ben is the UK's most iconic symbol. Since 2017, the Elizabeth Tower and the bell inside have been .....(1)..... renovation. The structure is 160 years old and .....(2)..... regular maintenance. ......(3).... many years, people had been painting the hands and numbers .....(4)..... the clock black, but last Thursday, the workers .....(5)..... the clock's original colour, Prussian Blue!

1. Select the most appropriate option for blank no. 1.
   (a) undermining
   (b) understanding
   (c) undergoing
   (d) undertaking

2. Select the most appropriate option for blank no. 2.
   (a) needs          (b) was needing
   (c) is needed      (d) had needed

3. Select the most appropriate option for blank no. 3.
   (a) About          (b) For
   (c) Before         (d) In

4. Select the most appropriate option for blank no. 4.
   (a) to             (b) of
   (c) at             (d) for

5. Select the most appropriate option for blank no. 5.
   (a) imparted       (b) invented
   (c) discovered     (d) concealed

### Passage II

Agatha Christie is a well known writer of mystery books. The ...(6)... in each of her stories involves everyday characters ...(7)... we can relate to. This makes her stories more ...(8)... because whatever she writes about can happen ...(9)... any of us. What makes her stories more interesting ...(10)... the twist at the end.

6. (a) style          (b) plot
   (c) title          (d) ending

7. (a) whose          (b) these
   (c) those          (d) that

8. (a) sarcastic      (b) realistic
   (c) artistic       (d) exotic

9. (a) to      (b) on      (c) by      (d) from

10. (a) was     (b) were    (c) are     (d) is

## Passage III

Bill Gates is the second-richest ....(11).... in the world. He is ...(12).... an estimated $ 103 billion. His wealth ....(13).... only by Jeff Bezos, ...(14)... has a current net worth of $ 116 billion. Gates is .....(15).... rich that an average American spending $1 is similar to Gates spending $ 1.6 million.

11. (a) person          (b) personnel
    (c) character       (d) human

12. (a) classes         (b) worth
    (c) valuable        (d) cost

13. (a) is surpassed    (b) surpasses
    (c) is surpassing   (d) surpassed

14. (a) which           (b) whose
    (c) whom            (d) who

15. (a) so    (b) too    (c) as    (d) such

## Passage IV

Trade on the New York Stock Exchange was ...(16).... to a standstill on an autumn day ...(17).... 1994. The culprit for the outage ...(18).... a squirrel that had chewed through a power line near the computer centre of the ...(19).... in Trumbull, Connecticut. The shutdown ...(20).... lasted for half an hour, resulted in the NYSE operating at 85 percent capacity.

16. (a) worked          (b) happened
    (c) taken           (d) brought

17. (a) in              (b) by
    (c) at              (d) on

18. (a) is              (b) were
    (c) was             (d) has

19. (a) town            (b) store
    (c) exchange        (d) bank

20. (a) which           (b) what
    (c) who             (d) whom

## Passage V

In July, 1937, the Japanese used an incident to provoke a war. They ...(21)... China and occupied a major portion ...(22)... it. Chinese and Japanese ...(23)... clashed in Northern China, throwing the entire country into ...(24)... . Millions of people were shot ...(25)... death.

21. (a) included        (b) extended
    (c) invaded         (d) persuaded

22. (a) for    (b) from    (c) of    (d) by

23. (a) caravans        (b) troops
    (c) mobs            (d) crowds

24. (a) turmoil         (b) peace
    (c) progress        (d) tranquility

25. (a) to    (b) in    (c) on    (d) for

# 2 Marks Questions

## Passage VI

26. People make plastic products by mixing the plastic with additives. The additives ...(i)... it difficult to recycle the plastic. To recycle plastic things, ...(ii)... grind them up first, but this new ...(iii)... is not easy to use again. A laboratory in California made a new type ...(iv)... plastic to deal with this problem. ...(v)... scientists put the new plastic in a high acid solution, the plastic and the additives break apart. People can then easily reuse the plastic.

(i) (a) make
    (b) makes
    (c) is making
    (d) was making

(ii)   (a) persons     (b) personnel
      (c) human beings
      (d) people

(iii)   (a) component   (b) thing
      (c) material     (d) object

(iv)   (a) to   (b) with   (c) in     (d) of

(v)   (a) But       (b) Until
      (c) When      (d) Then

## Passage VII

**27.** In one of the most high-profile localities in the capital, hundreds of ...**(i)**... walk across an unmanned railway track ...**(ii)**... day to get to school. Lakshman ...**(iii)**... his way down the rocky steps ...**(iv)**... lead to the railway track behind his settlement. He ...**(v)**... in the affirmative when asked if the track scares him. "I have fallen down these steps so many times during the monsoon. But there is no other way to walk to school", he says.

(i)   (a) men       (b) people
      (c) women     (d) children

(ii)   (a) each      (b) all
      (c) every      (d) whole

(iii)   (a) had made   (b) makes
      (c) was making (d) make

(iv)   (a) whom     (b) what
      (c) who       (d) which

(v)   (a) shakes     (b) salutes
      (c) nods       (d) winks

## Passage VIII

**28.** Every morning, nine-year old Khushi becomes guardian to her five year old sister Ankita as ...**(i)**... hold hands and cross the railway tracks to ...**(ii)**... the school. The sisters leave home ...**(iii)**... 7 am with school bags larger ...**(iv)**... their torsos. The 2 km route they walk on foot to reach school ...**(v)**... includes walking past a railway crossing and through the lanes of an industrial area used by mini trucks and carrier vehicles.

(i)   (a) them       (b) us
      (c) they       (d) we

(ii)   (a) reach      (b) arrive
      (c) go        (d) come

(iii)   (a) at    (b) on    (c) from   (d) in

(iv)   (a) than      (b) to
      (c) with      (d) from

(v)   (a) hardly     (b) daily
      (c) widely     (d) evenly

## Passage IX

**29.** Physical fitness is just as important for children as learning the letters and numbers. This realisation is not of recent ...**(i)**... . Most schools ...**(ii)**... a certain number of periods dedicated to physical activities. However, in the context of rising incidences of lifestyle related diseases ...**(iii)**... children and adolescents, the questions is, is this enought?

Before the ...**(iv)**... of televised distractions, children were often found outside the house playing in parks and even in the streets. But what really reduced playing time ...**(v)**... was the arrival and the rapid spread of the internet.

(i)   (a) origin      (b) organisation
      (c) origins     (d) organ

(ii)   (a) had       (b) have
      (c) having     (d) has

(iii)   (a) between    (b) into
      (c) among     (d) for

(iv)   (a) adventure   (b) adorning
      (c) evolution   (d) advent

(v)   (a) drastically   (b) hardly
      (c) marginaly    (d) closely

# Reading Comprehension

## 1 Mark Questions

**Directions** (Q. Nos. 1-5) Read the passage given below and answer the questions with the help of the options given below.

### Norway Mourns the Loss of Keiko

The killer whale, Keiko, who was the star of the film *Free Willy*, has died in a Norwegian fjord. He had always been a favourite with children and left the people of Halsa, his final home, distressed. After all the troubles in his life, he finally died of pneumonia. As the star of *Free Willy*, he leapt from a tank to freedom in the open sea. In real life, he did not escape so easily. Indeed, when the film was completed, he returned to the shallow water of a rusty tank in an aquarium near Mexico City.

Money was raised to help him and, after the film company Warner Brothers gave $5 million to the fund, he moved to Oregon, where he was nursed back to health. He even had a widescreen television to watch. Then he was flown to Iceland—the site of his original capture in 1978— and prepared for release into the ocean.

His handlers tried to break his bond with humankind and helped him learn how to catch fish. But he was not drawn to freedom and when he was lured out to sea, he simply followed the boat back to shore.

Finally, though, he joined a pod of killer whales and was tracked 800 miles across the Atlantic Ocean.

Nevertheless, seven weeks later, he arrived back in Europe, seeking human friends and frozen herring. He stayed in Halsa, Norway, where local children swam with him in the fjord. He seemed happy.

Unfortunately, fifteen months later Keiko died of pneumonia. It was ironic that he died of an illness usually associated with humans. And, of course, it is humans who mourn his passing, because he was loved by them, just as he loved humans in return.

1. What was so ironic about Keiko's death?
   - (a) He died in a Norwegian fjord.
   - (b) He died of an illness usually associated with humans.
   - (c) Humans mourned his death.
   - (d) He died after the film was completed.

2. Money was raised to help him because
   - (a) he lived in the shallow water of a rusty tank in an aquarium.
   - (b) he wanted a widescreen television to watch.
   - (c) he had no freedom in the tank.
   - (d) he needed medical aid to be nursed back to health.

3. What do you infer from the statement 'But he was not drawn to freedom'?
   - (a) He was not attracted to sea.
   - (b) He bonded well with humankind.
   - (c) He wanted to swim with local children in the fjord.
   - (d) He was very weak to enjoy his freedom.

4. Synonym of 'lured' is
   - (a) tempted     (b) deceived
   - (c) exerted     (d) persuaded

5. In the phrase 'break his bond' in the second paragraph, 'bond' here refers to
   - (a) rope, chain, or other restraints used to hold someone prisoner.
   - (b) a force or feeling that unites living beings.
   - (c) an agreement with legal force.
   - (d) a thing used to tie something or to fasten things together.

**Directions** (Q. Nos. 6-9) Read the passage given below and answer the questions with the help of the options given below.

Coco Chanel

Coco Chanel was born in 1883. She was famous for the clothes that she produced. Her clothes were revolutionary, quite unlike those that people wore at the time. Her ability to start new fashions made her one of the most successful designers of all time.

Coco Chanel's parents died when she was young. With her sister, she moved to Deauville in Northern France to work for a man who made and sold hats. In 1912, Chanel opened her own shop, but her hats were different. Instead of huge ones, decorated with fruit, feathers, bows and other trimmings, Chanel sold plain hats. She wore plain hats herself and simple, plain clothes.

In 1914, she opened a shop in Rue de Cambon in Paris. At that time, most women wore long skirts and corsets which restricted their movements. Chanel liked clothes which were easy to wear and which she could 'jump into'. Although she could not sew, she could pin and cut. Her styles were just right for independent women looking for greater freedom after World War I. She brought in all sorts of innovations to women's fashions, including cardigans, real pockets, artificial jewellery, Chanel No. 5 perfume and bell-bottomed trousers. She made a fortune from selling these things.

During World War II, Chanel remained in Paris and some people thought she was too friendly with the Germans who occupied France.

They expected her to lose her popularity after the war, but she remained as popular as ever by starting a new fashion revolution. Previously, she had sold things only to rich women. Now she made high fashion available to everyone. She produced thousands of copies of cheap but well-designed clothes.

6. The writer says 'Her clothes were revolutionary'. This means that Coco Channel's clothes were ........... .
   (a) unbelievably bright
   (b) strikingly attractive
   (c) totally different
   (d) truly simple

7. From the passage, the reader learns that Coco Chanel preferred to ........... .
   (a) work with her sister
   (b) sew her own clothes
   (c) wear fashions that were simple
   (d) design hats that were decorated

8. After World War I, Coco Chanel's styles were 'just right' for women who wanted to ........... .
   (a) make their own clothes
   (b) wear clothes similar to men's
   (c) look for more variety in their skirts and corsets
   (d) feel that they were free to dress as they liked

9. The word 'innovations' in the third paragraph means ........... .
   (a) new ideas
   (b) unusual items
   (c) expensive changes
   (d) unexpected additions

**Directions** (Q. Nos. 10-13) Read the poem given below and answer the questions with the help of the options given below.

### A Lady

*By Amy Lowell*

You are beautiful and faded
Like an old opera tune
Played upon a harpsichord;
Or like the sun-flooded silks
Of an eighteenth-century boudoir.
In your eyes
Smoulder the fallen roses of outlived minutes,
And the perfume of your soul

Is vague and suffusing,
With the pungence of sealed spice-jars.
Your half-tones delight me,
And I grow mad with gazing
At your blent colors.

My vigor is a new-minted penny,
Which I cast at your feet.
Gather it up from the dust,
That its sparkle may amuse you.

10. Which of the following is an example of a metaphor?
    (a) Like an old opera tune.
    (b) My vigor is a new-minted penny.
    (c) The perfume of your soul is vague and suffusing.
    (d) And I grow mad with gazing.

11. What do you infer about the subject of this poem?
    (a) This poem is about a vigorous young woman staring at an old lady.
    (b) This poem is about everyone waiting around at a retirement home.
    (c) This poem is about the appearance of an old lady.
    (d) This poem is about a beautiful and faded woman.

**12.** What is the mood of the poem?
(a) Violent        (b) Unhappy
(c) Still and calm     (d) Joyful

**13.** 'Vigor' as used in the poem means
(a) effort and enthusiasm
(b) energy and effort
(c) health and energy
(d) physical strength and good health

**Directions** (Q. Nos. 14-17) Read the poem given below and answer the questions with the help of the options given below.

### Operating Room

*By John Reed*

Sunlight floods the shiny many-windowed place,
Coldly glinting on flawless steel under glass,
And blaring imperially on the spattered gules
Where kneeling men grunt as they swab the floor.
Startled eyes of nurses swish by noiselessly,
Orderlies with cropped heads swagger like murderers;

And three surgeons, robed and masked mysteriously,
Lounge gossiping of guts, and wish it were lunch-time.

Beyond the porcelain door, screaming mounts crescendo.
Case 4001 coming out of the ether,
Born again half a man, to spend his life in bed.

**14.** What do you infer about the subject of this poem?
(a) This poem is about a man who will never walk again.
(b) This poem is about a man who will spend his life in bed.
(c) This poem is about an operating room in a hospital.
(d) This poem is about surgeons and patients.

**15.** How does the speaker treat the subject of the poem?
(a) With an objective and clinical callousness
(b) As a tragedy
(c) As a serious clinical matter
(d) With seriousness

**16.** 'To spend his life in bed' is an example of
(a) metaphor        (b) hyperbole
(c) oxymoron        (d) onomatopoeia

**17.** What is the mood of the poem?
(a) Violent and aggressive
(b) Sad, grim and depressing
(c) Calm and still
(d) Happy

## 2 Marks Questions

**Directions** (Q. Nos. 18-22) Read the passage given below and answer the questions with the help of the options given below.

### Cars of the Future

If Henry Ford, founder of Ford Motor Company, came back for a visit today, he would be amazed to see how cars have changed. When Ford manufactured cars in the early 1900s, the car had one purpose: to transport people from one place to another more quickly than in a horse and carriage. But in today's fast-paced world, a car must do much more than simply transport people. People want a car to provide comfort, efficiency, information and connection to the world.

Today, people of all ages spend many hours everyday in the car. Many people have to commute to work or school. They want to be able to do other things while they drive. Drivers want to be able to talk on the phone or get directions if they are lost. Passengers want to be able to watch videos or go online. Technology has already made these things possible.

What about cars of the future? The most exciting changes will be, thanks to the Internet, e.g. some cars already have a Global Positioning System or GPS. A GPS is a computerised system that gives directions to any place you want to go to. The directions are displayed on a small screen or can be "read" to you by the computer. But in the future, the GPS will be able to give you much more information. It can show you a map with different colours for different traffic conditions. Areas in red would mean traffic jams, purple would mean road construction, and blue would mean clear travelling. In addition, if you want to stop for a quick cup of coffee and a donut, you could ask your in-car computer.

It would tell you what restaurants are on your way, which ones have drive-through service, and which ones have the shortest lines. In the future, car computers will be able to understand what you say using voice-recognition software. You can say, "Call Frank Smith", and your computer will dial his number and connect you.

You can say, "Read my e-mail", and it will read your messages to you. And you will be able to dictate your replies and send them, while driving and watching the road. You can ask for directions, ask to change radio stations, or ask to change the temperature in the car. One of the most exciting systems being tested today is the "smartway". A smartway is a special lane of a highway for commuters. All cars in the smartway lane are controlled by a federal traffic computer. Cars are connected *via* the Internet. Cars are very close together, but are all travelling at the same speed. On the smartway, cars can go up to 100 miles per hour. Drivers will not have to steer or control their speed on the smartway. Their car will be on "autopilot", so drivers can sit back and relax. It is hard to imagine some of these changes in the future, but they are already being tested and developed. Someday, your commute to work may be a pleasure!

18. What do people want from a car today?
    (a) To commute from one place to another.
    (b) To provide comfort, efficiency, information and connection to the world while we travel.
    (c) To commute using GPS.
    (d) To drive on a smartway lane.

19. Which word can replace 'fast-paced' as used in the text?
    (a) Rapidly changing (b) Quick-paced
    (c) Fast-moving      (d) Fast-changing

20. What is a GPS?
    (a) a voice-recognition software
    (b) Computerised system that gives direction
    (c) Small screen to display direction
    (d) Most exciting system

21. What is the purpose of a smartway?
    (a) To control the cars using a federal traffic computer.
    (b) To connect the cars *via* internet.
    (c) To control the speed of all the cars in a way that all are travelling at the same speed.
    (d) To enable the car driver to sit back and relax.

**22.** Synonym of 'autopilot' is
   (a) gyropilot        (b) self pilot
   (c) automatic driver (d) robot pilot

**Directions** (Q. Nos. 23-27) Read the passage given below and answer the questions with the help of the options given below.

Should Technology Replace E-learning?

Gone are the days when one had to wait for a teacher to get back to you to clear your doubts. In this age of technology, we can learn things at any time, from any place. We need not wait to begin learning until the start of the semester.

E-learning has become popular around the world. A person sitting in a remote place can learn anything the world has to offer. Students belonging to different countries can learn the courses offered from a country they cannot afford to go to. Due to these advantages, e-learning has become the most opted form of learning these days.

What is the need for a teacher when a person can find things out for himself or herself? E-learning, after all, was devised such that educators' work is reduced. We don't really require someone lecturing about things. Through E-learning, the process of learning is revamped. It makes one feel independent.

Knowledge is just a click away. But does this mean we no longer require teachers? Of course not! E-learning is made easy because there are a set of learnt educators or teachers working together, putting in the data required and organising things, so that the person on the other end gets a hustle-free training session. You may think that you will be able to completely rely on technology to get the answers for all your questions. But the truth is that you will still require a guide to take you through the right path. At times, you may never be able to get the right answer and the searching will lead you into a loop wherein everything you get as an answer is not relevant.

In such cases, one requires a person who is knowledgeable to give you the correct answers, and that knowledgeable person is mostly a teacher who has done intensive study and research on the subject.

A system may crash at any time. You cannot rely on something that is virtual. E-learning is a virtual learning process. Just imagine you are interacting with "nobody". It is incomplete if there is nobody to update the data or guide you through properly or answer your queries as and when they occur.

Nothing can take over human intelligence or the teacher who shares knowledge without hesitating. No technology or man-made robot can ever replace the "old-reliable-teacher" who is just a call away to answer you, guide you and to help you out and most importantly, to be your motivator.

**23.** How has E-learning helped in the field of education?
   (a) Reduced the educator's work.
   (b) Revamped the process of learning.
   (c) Made one feel independent.
   (d) Reduced the dependence on teachers.

**24.** Which word can replace 'intensive' as used in the text?
   (a) Superficial       (b) Vigorous
   (c) Enough          (d) In-depth

**25.** Why can't we rely on E-learning?
   (a) It is a virtual learning process.
   (b) At times answers are not relevant.
   (c) The system may crash at any time.
   (d) All of the above

26. The expression 'just a call away' is an example of
    (a) idiom
    (b) colloquialism
    (c) jargon
    (d) cliche

27. Can E-learning replace teachers?
    (a) No. Nothing can take over human interaction.
    (b) Yes. Through E-learning knowledge is just a click away.
    (c) Yes. E-learning is made difficult because of teachers.
    (d) No. Teachers are important to guide, help and motivate.

**Directions** (Q. Nos. 28-32) Read the poem given below and answer the questions with the help of the options given below.

## The Fog

I saw the fog grow thick,
Which soon made blind my ken;
It made tall men of boys,
And giants of tall men.

> It clutched my throat, I coughed;
> Nothing was in my head
> Except two heavy eyes
> Like balls of burning lead.

And when it grew so black
That I could know no place
I lost all judgment then,
Of distance and of space.

> The street lamps, and the lights
> Upon the halted cars,
> Could either be on earth
> Or be the heavenly stars.

A man passed by me close,
I asked my way, he said,
"Come, follow me, my friend-"
I followed where he led.

He rapped the stones in front,
"Trust me", he said, "and come;"
I followed like a child-
A blind man led me home.

28. 'It clutched my throat, I coughed' tell us that
    (a) the poet was suffocating because of the fog.
    (b) the fog and the poet were fighting fiercely.
    (c) the fog held the poet by the throat.
    (d) the poet had a sore throat.

29. The following statements are true except
    (a) the fog grew so thick that the poet could not get his directions right.
    (b) a blind man who was also lost came to help the poet.
    (c) the fog caused the poet to see things differently.
    (d) the fog hurt the poet's eyes.

30. The word 'halted' shows that the cars were probably
    (a) stolen        (b) moving
    (c) expensive     (d) stationary

31. '… the stones in front' in the last stanza refers to
    (a) the stones the blind man carried in a pouch in front of him.
    (b) the stones that were lying by the side of the road.
    (c) the road they were on.
    (d) loose gravel.

32. We can infer from the poem that the blind man could lead the poet through the fog because he
    (a) was wearing a pair of glasses.
    (b) had been to the poet's house.
    (c) had a stick with him.
    (d) knew his way.

# Writing Skills

## 1 Mark Questions

**Directions** (Q. Nos. 1-10)In the following letter to the Editor, some words or parts of sentences are missing. Read the letter carefully and then complete the gaps by selecting the most appropriate option.

H. No. 2010,

Park Street,

New Delhi

15th July, 20XX

The Editor

The Hindustan Times,

KG Marg, New Delhi

Subject: ...(1)....

Sir

While circuses and travelling shows featuring wild animal acts may seem innocent enough, it has become apparent over the past decade that ...(2).... .

Most circuses and travelling shows that use wild animals keep them for months on end in cramped transport cages, sometimes hardly larger than they are, with only brief periods outside to perform. ...(3).... . That's why veterinarians, animal behaviourists, biologists and animal welfare organisations around the world have ...(4)... . Circuses and travelling shows with wild animals also ...(5).... . ...(6).... by performing animals, and circus audience members have been injured when handlers have lost control of their animals. Many performing animals are large, potentially dangerous species that even zoos don't handle.

...(7)...., they often do so without adequate protection for staff and audience members.

We now know that performing animals suffer in circuses and travelling shows and that wild animal acts pose a danger to human safety. ...(8)...., including entire countries, have recognised this and ...(9)....

Our community should not condone cruelty to animals by allowing performing animal acts to visit, nor should we wait for someone to be injured or killed before we decide to act in the interest of human safety. Thus, a prohibition on wild animal acts should be considered as soon as possible.

Thanking you

...(10)....

**Anand Tripathi**

*1.* (a) Wild Animals in the City
   (b) Danger to Animals
   (c) Performing Animals in the City
   (d) Ban the Animals

*2.* (a) wild animals are cruel
   (b) wild animal acts are inherently cruel and unsafe
   (c) animals are treated wildly
   (d) animals are misused

*3.* (a) The animals have no opportunity to move or behave in a natural way
   (b) The animals enjoy themselves
   (c) The animals have an opportunity to entertain themselves
   (d) The animals act even more violently

*4.* (a) encouraged wild animal acts
   (b) shown interest in wild animal acts
   (c) supported wild animal acts
   (d) condemned wild animal acts

*5.* (a) pose a risk to human safety
   (b) endanger other lives
   (c) make huge profits
   (d) generate vacancies for the needy

*6.* (a) Numerous circus employees have become rich
   (b) Numerous circus employees have been seriously injured or killed
   (c) Hardly a few employees have been injured
   (d) Many employees have performed daring acts

*7.* (a) But when they perform at home
   (b) They perform for money but
   (c) But when they do not perform
   (d) But when they perform in circuses and travelling shows

*8.* (a) Hundreds of places around the world
   (b) Law around the nation
   (c) Legal rules around the world
   (d) Hundreds of circus authorities

*9.* (a) encouraged wild animals acts
   (b) raised their voice for the same
   (c) prohibited wild animal acts
   (d) banned circus shows

*10.* (a) Your's obediently (b) Yours sincerely
   (c) Yours lovingly     (d) Your's sincerely

**Directions** (Q. Nos. 11-20) In the following letter to a friend, some words or sentences are missing. Read the letter carefully and then complete the gaps by selecting the most appropriate option.

H.No. 462,
Mall Road,
Manali

...(**11**)...

Dear Aakash

...(**12**)..., which arrived this morning. It was really my turn to write, as you say, ...(**13**)... . I mean, life goes on as always, and ...(**14**)... . Last weekend was fun, though.

As you may remember, it was Aanchal's birthday, last Saturday and ...(**15**)....
...(**16**)..., she decided to have a midnight picnic in Glover Wood. ...(**17**)...? Just beside the old fort.

Well, anyway, we all met at the Red Coral, had a few snacks there, and then went on down to the Glover Wood. ...(**18**)..., so we were able to make our way there without much trouble. As you can imagine, there was a great deal of messing about when we got there-people shouting and chasing each other around, and so on. But when we started eating, the noise died down. It was then that we suddenly became aware of the stillness of the night and although it sounds odd to say so, ...(**19**)... we had been making before.

All in all, it was an unforgettable experience. I'm sure Aanchal's picnic will be talked about for sometime.

Well, nothing more to tell you just now; ...(**20**)...

Yours lovingly

Shruti

11. (a) Aanchal's picnic
    (b) 27th November, 20XX
    (c) To, House no. 788, Mall Road, Shimla
    (d) India

12. (a) Do you know that your letter
    (b) I was expecting your letter
    (c) Thank you very much for your letter
    (d) I received your letter

13. (a) but I seem to have so little news these days
    (b) but I was in no mood to write
    (c) but I almost forgot
    (d) but I was angry at you

14. (a) we do forget small things in life
    (b) we are too preoccupied with other important stuff
    (c) we forget our unimportant friends
    (d) nothing special seems to happen

15. (a) she wanted to do something different
    (b) she did not want to celebrate
    (c) she wanted to go camping
    (d) she wanted to sleep all day

16. (a) Instead of sleeping all day
    (b) Instead of celebrating
    (c) Instead of cutting the birthday cake
    (d) Instead of the usual party at home

17. (a) Have you forgotten it
    (b) You remember it, don't you
    (c) I bet you haven't seen it
    (d) You must have forgotten it

18. (a) There were footprints all over the ground
    (b) Because we were all together
    (c) Fortunately, there was a bright moon
    (d) We all went in different directions

19. (a) the silence seemed even louder than the noise
    (b) the darkness of the night reduced the noise
    (c) the ghostly figures appeared and reduced the noise
    (d) strange sounds scared us and the noise was more than

20. (a) hope you sleep well
    (b) hope to see you at Christmas
    (c) hope to scare you more in future
    (d) hope to have you replied

**Directions** (Q. Nos. 21-25) Given below is a notice with incomplete information. Read it carefully and then answer the questions that follow by choosing the most appropriate option.

---

ABC SCHOOL, DELHI

**NOTICE**

12th January, 20XX

........(**21**).......

........(**22**)......... all students of Class X that a three day workshop from 9th to 11th February on 'Acquired Immuno Deficiency Syndrome' will be conducted in the ........(**23**)......... by teachers from DPS Noida from ........(**24**).......... everyday. Attendance is compulsory.

Arun Arora

........(**25**)..........

---

21. The heading of the notice should be ............... .
    (a) AIDS
    (b) Workshop on AIDS
    (c) Let's Fight AIDS
    (d) Seminar on AIDS

22. The appropriate beginning for the notice is ............... .
    (a) The school is organising for
    (b) This notice informs

(c) All the students are informed that

(d) This is to inform

23. The appropriate venue for the workshop can be ............... .
    (a) canteen
    (b) gym area
    (c) conference hall
    (d) playground

24. Duration of the workshop: ............... .
    (a) Monday to Sunday
    (b) 9 am to 11 am
    (c) 2 hours
    (d) Morning to evening

25. Designation: ...............
    (a) Principal          (b) Head Boy
    (c) Head Girl          (d) Supervisor

**Directions** (Q. Nos 26-30) Given below is a notice with incomplete information. Read it carefully and fill in the missing information by selecting the most appropriate option.

---

........(26).........

**NOTICE**

**23rd February, 20XX**

.........(27)..........

.........(28)........ is organising a Holi bash in the colony as per the following details :

**Date :** 27th February, 20XX

**Time :** 9 am to 5 pm

..........(29).........

The residents are requested to come along with their families and friends and add colour to the rejoicing.

Ravi Kumar

.........(30).........

---

26. (a) ABC School, Patna
    (b) Residents Welfare Association
    (c) ABC Housing Society
    (d) Resident's Welfare Association

27. (a) Festival Time     (b) Get Together
    (c) Meeting           (d) Holi Fiesta

28. (a) The society
    (b) The general body of society
    (c) The Resident's Welfare Association
    (d) The residents

29. (a) DAY : Monday
    (b) WIN : Free Gifts
    (c) Venue : Green Park Club
    (d) Note : Kids not Allowed

30. (a) Resident
    (b) Neighbour
    (c) President, RWA
    (d) Outsider

**Direction** (Q. Nos 31-35) Given below is a notice making an appeal for generous donations. However, you will find some mistakes. Read it carefully and replace the underlined mistakes, by selecting the most appropriate option.

---

ST . MARKS HIGH SCHOOL, SHIMLA

**NOTICE**

6th October, 20XX

**31.** Attention!

Your **32.** attention are required to make a difference in the lives of the **33.** rich and wealthy living in the state run homes. Donate generously. Deposit your contribution to the undersigned by **34.** next year. The money so raised will be spent on **35.** lavish lifestyle for the residents.

Ram Dhavan

Head Boy

---

31. (a) Attention Please!
    (b) Make an Appeal
    (c) Lend a Helping Hand
    (d) Cooperate Please!

**32.** (a) help and cooperation
    (b) peace and union
    (c) prayers and faith
    (d) money and funds

**33.** (a) poor
    (b) less fortunate
    (c) moderate population
    (d) dead

**34.** (a) today
    (b) canteen
    (c) school library
    (d) 15th October, 20XX

**35.** (a) medicines and clothes
    (b) making difference
    (c) donations
    (d) making appeals

# 2 Marks Questions

**Directions** (Q. Nos 36-40) Following is a diary entry. Some words and phrases are missing. Read the diary entry carefully and complete the missing information by selecting the most appropriate option.

11th March, 20XX

.........(36)..........

10:40 pm

Dear Diary

Holi has come and gone. I now have red ears, yellow cheeks and hands, a blue neck and a magenta scalp. It will take many more baths .........(37)........... .

We had so much fun today. There were sweets, a fabulous lunch and lots of games. The crowning point was the dunking in a tub full of coloured water! I danced like mad and sprayed .........(38)............ . I was a sheer terror to women and children, who screamed and ran when they saw me coming. But none escaped. Only Didi, silly girl, slapped me because .........(39)........... . Dad gave me five hundred rupees for .........(40).......... Now, what should I buy? May be a new video game. However, if I can get another five hundred from mom, then I can buy something really cool-may be, like the Formula - 1 model race-track and cars. Wow!

Aman

**36.** (a) Yesterday     (b) Today
    (c) Past midnight   (d) Saturday

**37.** (a) before my skin returns to normal
    (b) to wash off the skin
    (c) before I could go to school
    (d) to shine again

**38.** (a) balloon on everyone
    (b) ink on everyone
    (c) colours on everyone
    (d) water-colours on none

**39.** (a) I threw her in the tub
    (b) I sprayed colour in her eyes
    (c) I slapped her
    (d) I attacked her with eggs

**40.** (a) not damaging the car
    (b) throwing all the girls in the tub
    (c) sharing my colours with him
    (d) sharing my secret with him

**Directions** (Q. Nos 41-45) Following is a diary entry. Some words and phrases are missing. Read the diary entry carefully and complete the missing information by selecting the most appropriate option.

9th April, 20XX

Thursday

9:15 pm

Dear Diary

.........(41).......... . While walking home from school, I saw a man selling parrots in cages. I must say they were exceptionally beautiful.

.........(42)........., I stopped there and picked up the most talkative one. I was so glad and excited. I thought of feeding it green chillies. I also planned to teach it to speak. When I showed it to mother, .........(43).......... . Although she did not object, she handed me a book of poems.

As I began to read, I came across a poem about birds flying in the open sky. It changed my mind drastically and .........(44).......... . Mother was very happy and kissed my forehead. .........(45).......... . I was very happy to see my parrot free from confinement.

*Shourya*

41. (a) Something was different
    (b) Something unusual happened today
    (c) Today was a monotonous day
    (d) I enjoyed the day today

42. (a) Tempted to buy one
    (b) Aghast at the sight
    (c) I was so shocked that
    (d) Unable to avoid

43. (a) she was very angry
    (b) she left the house
    (c) she was totally surprised
    (d) she slapped me

44. (a) I gave him cake to eat
    (b) I opened the cage and set my little friend free in the open sky
    (c) I put the cage in the balcony
    (d) I hanged the little cage in fresh air

45. (a) I felt a sense of frustration
    (b) I felt bad for hurting her feelings
    (c) I felt that she has forgiven me
    (d) I felt a sense of relief and contentment

**Directions** (Q. Nos 46-55) In the following article, some words and phrases are missing. Complete the missing words and phrases by selecting the most appropriate option.

### Cyber Crime

.......(46).........

The rapid growth of the internet and computer technology over the past few years has led to the growth in new forms of ......(47)......... throughout the world.

Cyber crime is defined as crimes committed on the internet using computer as a tool and we innocents are the target. There are various forms of cyber crime, like spamming. I am sure all of us have encountered ......(48)...... . Piracy is also a serious threat that involves ........(49)...... of software applications, games, movies and audio CDs, which is causing a huge monetary loss to entertainment industry worldwide. Hacking is also a serious crime by a hacker who is simply a talented computer user, who ........(50)....... . Virus attacks that say "I love you" enter our computer and destroy all the computer information are also a serious threat. Computer frauds, thefts and harassments through .......(51)........ like Facebook and Twitter are also endangering our lives. Undoubtedly, we cannot single out only one crime that is posing the maximum threat, but all forms of crimes are equally posing a serious threat to both ......(52)..........

Moreover, IT experts should be recruited into law enforcement agencies to assist in the fight. At this hour when cyber crime is growing .......(53)........ with growing technology, the government needs to strengthen criminal penalties against computer crimes, work to harmonise laws against cyber crime internationally, and improve coordination among law enforcement authorities in different jurisdictions.

Consequently, there will always be new and unexpected challenges to stay ahead of .......(54)........, but we can win only through ......(55)........ between individuals and the government.

46. (a) And its effects
    (b) By Anaira
    (c) A serious threat
    (d) None

47. (a) cyber world
    (b) cyber criminals
    (c) criminal activities
    (d) crime-dubbed cyber crime

48. (a) unwanted product advertisements
    (b) spams
    (c) dubious mails
    (d) intrusion into our junk mails

49. (a) legal ways of distributing
    (b) illegal reproduction and distribution
    (c) making copies
    (d) sale and distribution

50. (a) is proud of his skills
    (b) is a boon to terrorists
    (c) is born to threaten the cyber security
    (d) misuses his vast knowledge

51. (a) common sites
    (b) popular sites
    (c) social networking sites
    (d) social sites

52. (a) world and individual
    (b) countries and nations
    (c) rich and the poor
    (d) businesses and individuals

53. (a) by leaps and bounds
    (b) manifolds
    (c) at a wanted speed
    (d) in innumerable ways

54. (a) criminals and terrorists
    (b) cyber criminals and cyber terrorists
    (c) cyber crime
    (d) criminal activities

55. (a) partnership and collaboration
    (b) mutual understanding
    (c) union
    (d) common thinking

**Directions** (Q. Nos 56-65) In the following article, some parts of sentences are incorrect. These have been underlined. Read the article carefully and then replace the incorrect parts by selecting the most appropriate option.

### Beggary Business

*By Saransh Sharma*

Beggary is an issue of **56.** privilege. Bus stops, crossings, streets and roads are **57.** neat and clean. Small children, men and women ask for money or food from **58.** the world.

They sometimes disturb traffic. Beggars generally approach foreigners, tourists or newcomers to the city. They create a very **59.** impressive impression on outsiders. Moreover, it is not due to **60.** poverty that people beg. Often they make it their business. Hence, we need to stop promoting beggary by **61.** threatening beggars completely.

Beggary is a **62.** blessing for the development of the country. Beggars are **63.** skilful people which are wasted and do not contribute in any way to the development of the country. Hence, beggars need to be **64.** encouraged and thus, the **65.** upliftment of beggars will come to an end.

56. (a) proud moment
    (b) serious problem
    (c) nation's hindrance
    (d) national shame

57. (a) full of stray animals
    (b) full of nomads
    (c) full of beggars
    (d) full of physically-challenged people

58. (a) passers-by          (b) pedestrians
    (c) foreigners          (d) tourists

59. (a) positive impression
    (b) bad impression
    (c) tempting impression
    (d) challenging

60. (a) financial problems
    (b) business
    (c) unemployment
    (d) forced circumstances

61. (a) helping beggars
    (b) employing beggars
    (c) ignoring beggars
    (d) scolding beggars

62. (a) boon
    (b) turnover
    (c) only solution
    (d) curse

63. (a) innocent poor people
    (b) unproductive human resources
    (c) unwanted human race
    (d) hardworking human race

64. (a) uplifted          (b) discouraged
    (c) employed          (d) empowered

65. (a) poverty problem
    (b) business of beggary
    (c) cause of beggary
    (d) beggars

# Communication Skills

## 1 Mark Questions

**Directions** (Q. Nos. 1-14) Choose the best response to the following from the given options.

**1.** Sukriti: Where did you keep my note book?

Kiran:
(a) How do I know?
(b) You can make a guess.
(c) Sorry, I haven't seen it.
(d) You should be knowing

**2.** Commuter to Fellow Commuter: Where is the exit for this metro station?

Fellow Commuter :
(a) Are you illiterate?
(b) Please take left and then right for the exit.
(c) Please don't distrub me.
(d) Follow me and you will know.

**3.** Rimpy: Is it ABC Enterprises?

Receptionist:
(a) Why have you called?
(b) This is not the right time to call.
(c) Don't ever call on this number again.
(d) Yes, How may I help you?

**4.** Shubham: I met with an accident today.

Princy:
(a) You deserve it.
(b) Oh! Sorry to hear that.

(c) Why are you always so careless?
(d) Your party is due. Isn't it?

**5.** Pragya: Can you share your notes with me, Rahul? I was absent for two days.

Rahul:
(a) Yes, sure. For which subject do you want?
(b) I don't take notes.
(c) No way.
(d) You may watch the online videos of the classes you have missed.

**6.** Parul: I invite you to my birthday party tomorrow at 5 PM.

Shekhar:
(a) Thanks for the invitation.
(b) I'm not interested.
(c) Why don't you invite Rohan in place of me?
(d) I don't like to attend birthday parties, you know?

**7.** Student: I'm having difficulty in joining the online class.

Coordinator:
(a) Ask your parents to do it for you.
(b) Your phone may be outdated. You better purchase a new one.
(c) Ok, Do you get any error message when you try to join it?
(d) You' re good for nothing.

**8.** Patient: How do I register to get the corona vaccine?

Nurse:

(a) Please download the Co-Win App and register on it.

(b) We don't have any information about it.

(c) Wait, You'll get automatically registered.

(d) Give me your mobile phone for a minute.

**9.** Sonam: Look out or you will hit your head.

Nupur:

(a) I don't care.

(b) Don't disturb me.

(c) Look who's talking.

(d) Thanks, That was just in time.

**10.** Prajwal: I've won the online painting contest. I'm flying to Bengaluru to get the award.

Seema:

(a) Oh!

(b) How did you manage to win it?

(c) Great! Many congratulations to you.

(d) Hmmm...

**11.** Father: Come, let's go for a walk.
Daughter:

(a) Well! It's too dark now.

(b) Please take mother along with you.

(c) I'm very tired. Please excuse me.

(d) I can't go in these clothes.

**12.** Rishabh: I've dropped my father's laptop. He will scold me. What shall I do?

Naman:

(a) You're in deep trouble.

(b) Just keep quiet about it.

(c) I'm glad I'm not in your shoes!

(d) Tell him about it. He'll understand.

**13.** Patient: I have an MRI scan scheduled for tomorrow. Could you please reschedule it for day after tomorrow as I have to attend an urgent meeting?

Receptionist:

(a) You should've informed earlier.

(b) I'm sorry. There are no slots available for day after tomorrow. Please suggest some other date.

(c) Ok! I will reschedule it if you give ₹ 500 to me.

(d) You may attend your meeting if it's that important.

**14.** Ankita: I don't know how I will be able to complete my project?

Gaurav:

(a) You can get it made from a shop in Lajpat Nagar.

(b) Don't panic. Go step by step and ask me if you need help.

(c) I knew very well that you'll be unable to complete it.

(d) Don't take tension. Inform your teacher that it's too tough for you.

# 2 Marks Questions

**Directions** (Q. Nos. 15 and 16) Each of the following conversations has mixed up sentences. Reorder them correctly and choose the correct option.

**15.** A. It was not so good.

B. What happened?

C. How was your trip?

D. I lost my bag.

(a) C - A - B - D     (b) A - B - D - C

(c) D - B - C - A     (d) A - D - C - B

**16.** A. Which bus goes to Tilak Nagar from here?

B. Go to the play store and download it.

C. I don't know. You can check it on the One Delhi App.

    D. It's not in my phone.
    (a) A - C - B - D     (b) A - C - D - B
    (c) D - B - C - A     (d) C - A - B - D

**Directions** (Q. Nos. 17-23) Choose the most appropriate response for the following situations.

**17.** What is the best way to ask someone to repeat something?

    A. You're speaking too fast. Slow down.

    B. Could you say that again, please?

    C. You better repeat what you said.

    D. I didn't get a word you said.

    **Codes**

    (a) Only A     (b) Only B
    (c) Both C and D     (d) Both A and B

**18.** Someone thanks you for helping him/her out. What will you say?

    A. You're welcome.

    B. Don't mention it.

    C. You can return my favour.

    D. It's okay.

    **Codes**

    (a) Both A and C     (b) Both B and D
    (c) A, B and C     (d) Both A and B

**19.** You're the conductor of a local bus. One of the passengers is not wearing a mask. How will you urge him/her to wear one?

    A. Get down or wear a mask.

    B. How dare you enter the bus without wearing a mask?

    C. Please borrow a mask from someone and wear it.

    D. Please wear your mask.

    **Codes**

    (a) Only C     (b) Both A and B
    (c) Both C and D     (d) Only D

**20.** You happen to meet your friend after years. Your response will be

    A. Great to see you after ages!

    B. Oh! What are you doing here?

    C. Hmm... I don't know you.

    D. I'm in a hurry, will catch you later.

    **Codes**

    (a) Only A     (b) Both B and D
    (c) Only C     (d) None of these

**21.** You're going to be late to meet your friend. Which of the following is the appropriate message to tell him/her that you're late?

    A. Have a snack while you wait for me.

    B. Aargh! Traffic is really bad. I'll be more than 10 mins late.

    C. I hope you're having a great time.

    D. You're used to waiting for me, aren't you?

    **Codes**

    (a) Only C     (b) Only B
    (c) Both B and C     (d) Both A and D

**22.** Your cousin has invited you for an outing. Somehow, you will be unable to attend it. The best way to turn down his invitation is

    A. to not inform him/her that you'll be unable to come.

    B. Sorry! I have other plans. I'll definitely go next time.

    C. I wish I could make it, but I have a test that day.

    D. I won't come as its too hot.

    **Codes**

    (a) Only C     (b) Only D
    (c) Both A and C     (d) Both B and C

**23.** Your uncle has booked a railway ticket for you as your internet was not working. Which of the following is the appropriate message for thanking him to help you out?

    A. I will call you again if I need help.

    B. Thanks a lot, uncle. I appreciate your help.

    C. You're my best uncle.

    D. You always help me when I need it.

    **Codes**

    (a) Only D     (b) Only B
    (c) Both B and D     (d) Both A and C

Chapter

# 16

# Verbal Ability

## 1 Mark Questions

**Directions** (Q. Nos. 1 and 2) Choose the correct option that you conclude by reading the paragraphs given below in each question.

**1.** Vincent has a paper route. Each morning, he delivers 37 newspapers to customers in his neighbourhood. It takes Vincent 50 minutes to deliver all the papers. If Vincent is sick or has other plans, his friend Thomas, who lives on the same street, will sometimes deliver the papers for him.

Which of the following statements is true?

(a) Vincent and Thomas live in the same neighbourhood.

(b) It takes Thomas more than 50 minutes to deliver the papers.

(c) It is dark outside when Vincent begins his deliveries.

(d) Thomas would like to have his own paper route.

**2.** Erin is twelve years old. For three years, she has been asking her parents for a dog. Her parents have told her that they believe a dog would not be happy in an apartment, but they have given her permission to have a bird. Erin has not yet decided what kind of bird she would like to have.

Which of the following statements is true?

(a) Erin's parents like birds better than they like dogs.

(b) Erin does not like birds.

(c) Erin and her parents live in an apartment.

(d) Erin and her parents would like to move.

**Directions** (Q. Nos. 3 and 4) Each question below consists of three statements. Based on the first two statements, the third statement may be true, false or uncertain. Choose the right option.

**3.** I. Blueberries cost more than strawberries.

II. Blueberries cost less than raspberries.

III. Raspberries cost more than both strawberries and blueberries.

If the first two statements are true, the third statement is

(a) true       (b) false

(c) uncertain       (d) None of these

**4.** I. All the tulips in Zoe's garden are white.

II. All the pansies in Zoe's garden are yellow.

III. All the flowers in Zoe's garden are either white or yellow.

If the first two statements are true, the third statement is

(a) true       (b) false

(c) uncertain       (d) None of these

**Directions** (Q. Nos. 5 and 6) In the following questions, a statement is given followed by two assumptions numbered I and II. You have to consider the statement and the following assumptions and decide which of the assumptions is implicit in the statement.

5. **Statement** Ministry has announced an economic package to support voluntary organisations— an official notice.

   **Assumptions**

   I. Voluntary organisations do not need such support.

   II. Government was not supporting voluntary organisations earlier.

   (a) Only assumption I is implicit
   (b) Only assumption II is implicit
   (c) Either I or II is implicit
   (d) Neither I nor II is implicit

6. **Statement** Detergents should be used to clean clothes.

   **Assumptions**

   I. Detergents form more lather.

   II. Detergents help to dislodge grease and dirt.

   (a) Only assumption I is implicit
   (b) Only assumption II is implicit
   (c) Either I or II is implicit
   (d) Neither I nor II is implicit

7. A is the brother of B; B is the sister of C; and C is the father of D. How is D related to A?

   (a) Brother
   (b) Sister
   (c) Nephew
   (d) Cannot be determined

8. Introducing a boy, a girl said, "He is the son of the only daughter of the father of my only uncle". How is the boy related to the girl?

   (a) Brother        (b) Nephew
   (c) Uncle          (d) Son-in-law

9. Amit said, "This girl is the wife of the grandson of my mother". How is Amit related to the girl?

   (a) Brother        (b) Grandfather
   (c) Husband        (d) Father-in-law

10. Deepak said to Nitin, "That boy playing with the football is the younger of the two brothers of the daughter of my father's wife". How is the boy playing football related to Deepak?

    (a) Son            (b) Brother
    (c) Cousin         (d) Brother-in-law

**Directions** (Q. Nos. 11-20) Choose the most appropriate option for the following.

11. You come to know about the demise of your best friend's mother.
    You will .........
    (a) go to his/her place and offer your condolences.
    (b) go to meet him/her but act as if you don't know anything.
    (c) ignore the news and continue with your work.
    (d) make a video call and talk to him/her.

12. You are travelling in the metro and find that the passenger sitting next to you has got down (deboarded) at the last station but has forgot one of her bags.
    You will ............
    (a) take her bag with you.
    (b) open the bag and take out the things that you like.
    (c) ignore the incident.
    (d) raise an alarm and inform the metro staff about the incident.

13. You have an online exam scheduled for tomorrow.
    Your laptop breaks down and you have no other means to take the exam.
    You will .......

(a) inform your teacher about the situation and request her to postpone the exam.

(b) skip the exam.

(c) arrange a laptop from a friend/relative for taking the exam.

(d) Both (a) and (c).

14. You get stuck in a traffic jam and as a result you are late for your final exam.
    You will ............

    (a) request the invigilator to give you extra time after explaining the situation to him/her.

    (b) take the exam half-heartedly.

    (c) take the exam and do what you can in the remaining time.

    (d) skip the exam.

15. You purchase a video game online. When it is delivered, you find that it is not functioning properly.
    You will ............

    (a) try to fix the issue yourself.

    (b) get it repaired from a mechanic near your house.

    (c) call the customer care department of the online store to lodge a complaint.

    (d) call the police to inform about the faulty video game.

16. You find that a stranger is walking around the compound of your residential complex.
    What will you do?

    (a) Remain engaged in your work.

    (b) Inform the guard of your residential complex.

    (c) Inform the police about the issue.

    (d) Catch the person and ask him/her about his/her motive.

17. You are waiting for your school bus. You withness an accident in which a biker falls off his bike and is lying unconscious on the road.

What is the best way to respond to this situation?

    (a) Give first aid to the injured biker and take him to the nearest hospital.

    (b) Let the biker lie where he is and take a ride on his bike till your school bus arrives.

    (c) Keep waiting for your school bus.

    (d) Click a photo of the accident site and share it with your friends.

18. You burn your hand while you are making tea.
    You will ............

    (a) put a band-aid on the burn.

    (b) apply ointment on the burnt hand.

    (c) put the hand in cold water for sometime.

    (d) put the hand in hot water for sometime.

19. Your best friend has scored better marks than you in the final exam.
    You will ........

    (a) congratulate him/her on his/her success and keep working hard for the next exam.

    (b) get demotivated and stop studying.

    (c) stop talking to him/her.

    (d) tell your parents that the teacher favours him/ her and hence has awarded him/her more marks.

20. You have scored very low marks in your unit test.
    You will ............

    (a) tell your parents that the result has not been declared yet.

    (b) change the marks and share the fake report card with your parents.

    (c) Inform your parents about your bad performance and promise to work hard in the future.

    (d) tell your parents that there has been some mistake in checking your papers.

# 2 Marks Questions

**Directions** (Q. Nos. 21-25) Choose the most appropriate option for the following.

21. You appear in an exam and notice that most of the questions in the exam are out of syllabus. You point out this issue to the invigilator and she tells you that she can't do anything.
What will you do?
    (a) Walk out of the examination hall.
    (b) Attempt the exam to the best of your ability.
    (c) Use unfair means to solve the out of syllabus questions.
    (d) Inform other candidates to boycott the exam.

22. You have been asked to deliver a small speech by your class teacher in the morning assembly. Before giving the speech on the designated day, you are feeling very anxious and think that you would not be able to do it.
You will ........
    (a) ask your best friend to give the speech on your behalf.
    (b) calm yourself down by taking a few deep breaths and deliver the speech.
    (c) give an excuse to your teacher and request to find a substitute for delivering the speech.
    (d) absent yourself form school.

23. A friend from a different religious community has invited you to attend a religious function at his/her home.
You will .......
    (a) decline the invitation stating that you do not share his/her religious beliefs.
    (b) accept the invitation but send him/her a message at the last minute regarding your inability to attend.
    (c) accept the invitation and join the function and invite him/her to such functions at your place in future.
    (d) accept the invitation and join the function but do not invite him/her at such functions that are held at your place.

24. You are getting a burning smell in your house. You check the cooking gas and cylinder and find out that there is no leakage.
What is going to be your next step?
    (a) Open the windows.
    (b) Ignore the smell and continue with what you were doing.
    (c) Switch off all the electric equipments and restart them after 5 minutes.
    (d) Switch off the mains and call an electrician to check the issue.

25. A student of your class has a habit of bullying the weaker students of your class when the teacher is not around.
You will ..........
    (a) complain to the teacher about the student's activities.
    (b) join the student in bullying the other students.
    (c) tell the student assertively that bullying is wrong and ask him/her to stop indulging in it.
    (d) get the support of your friends and start teasing the student who is a bully.

# PRACTICE SET 01

## 1 Mark Questions

**1.** Select the collective noun from the following.
   - (a) Gentry
   - (b) Hillock
   - (c) Apostle
   - (d) Carnage

**2.** Which of the following is a concrete noun?
   - (a) Disregard
   - (b) Perfume
   - (c) Generation
   - (d) Dexterity

**Directions** (Q. Nos. 3-5) Choose the odd one out from the following.

**3.** (a) Significance
   - (b) Nomenclature
   - (c) Plurality
   - (d) Significant

**4.** (a) Pansy
   - (b) Holistic
   - (c) Nocturnal
   - (d) Garrulous

**5.** (a) Chamber
   - (b) Creek
   - (c) Abdicate
   - (d) Elf

**6.** Which of the following is not a pronoun?
   - (a) Its
   - (b) One
   - (c) Each other
   - (d) It's

**Directions** (Q. Nos. 7 and 8) Choose the correct one word substitution for the following.

**7.** One who runs away from justice.
   - (a) Alarmist
   - (b) Fastidious
   - (c) Fugitive
   - (d) Fatalist

**8.** A religious war
   - (a) Carnage
   - (b) Crusade
   - (c) Parable
   - (d) Potable

**9.** Some part of the following sentence have been jumbled up. Rearrange these parts which are labelled as P, Q, R and S to produce the correct sentence.

Nelson Mandela
   P. modern country in a modern way
   Q. and could run a new
   R. shifted the beliefs of the people
   S. so they could heal the racial conflict
   - (a) RPSQ
   - (b) PQRS
   - (c) SRQP
   - (d) RSQP

**10.** Fill in the blank with an appropriate preposition.
   She scrambled from ......... the wagon and hastily threw her blankets under the seat.
   - (a) below
   - (b) under
   - (c) underneath
   - (d) over

**11.** Which of the following does not collocate properly?
   - (a) Problem stretching
   - (b) Annual turnover
   - (c) Takeover bid
   - (d) Customer friendly

**12.** Find the adjectives in the following sentence.
   Prajakta did her formal schooling from a government school and then enrolled herself in a professional course.
   - (a) Formal
   - (b) Formal, Professional
   - (c) Professional, Government
   - (d) Formal, Government, Professional

**Directions** (Q. Nos 13 and 14) Choose the correct meaning of the underlined idioms in the sentences from the given options.

13. Komal was <u>left high and dry</u> by her friends when she lost all her money.
    - (a) Isolated
    - (b) Rejected
    - (c) Wounded
    - (d) Depressed

14. It was such a strange affair that I was unable to <u>make head or tail of</u> it.
    - (a) Face it
    - (b) Tolerate it
    - (c) Remember it
    - (d) Understand it

**Directions** (Q. Nos. 15 and 16) Choose the correct synonym of the underlined words in the given sentences.

15. The five experiments conducted by Shivani gave <u>disparate</u> results.
    - (a) Similar
    - (b) Encouraging
    - (c) Strange
    - (d) Different

16. Our teacher followed a <u>devious</u> route to her destination.
    - (a) Difficult
    - (b) Winding
    - (c) Straight
    - (d) Short-cut

17. Choose the correct antonym of the underlined word in the given sentence.

    Savita made a <u>fervent</u> appeal to the members of the club to maintain unity.
    - (a) Active
    - (b) Apathetic
    - (c) Loud
    - (d) Passionate

**Directions** (Q. Nos. 18 and 19) Choose the correct indirect speech of the following sentences.

18. Pratham said to the servant, "If you don't wash the clothes properly, I will dismiss you".
    - (a) Pratham warned the servant that he would dismiss her if she didn't wash the clothes properly.
    - (b) Pratham told the servant that he would dismiss her on the event of bad work.
    - (c) Pratham cautioned the servant that she must wash the clothes properly.
    - (d) Pratham advised the servant to wash the clothes properly.

19. Kiran asked, "Did you see the cricket match on TV last night?"
    - (a) Kiran asked me whether I saw the cricket match on TV the earlier night.
    - (b) Kiran asked me whether I had seen the cricket match on TV the earlier night.
    - (c) Kiran asked me did I see the cricket match on TV last night.
    - (d) Kiran asked me whether I had seen the cricket match on TV last night.

**Directions** (Q. Nos. 20-25) Choose the part of the sentence that contains an error. If there is no error, mark option (d) i.e. 'No error' as your answer.

20. Several of the letters typed by Naina, the new secretary, they were full of mistakes.
    - (a) Several of the letters
    - (b) typed by Naina, the new secretary,
    - (c) they were full of mistakes
    - (d) No error

21. Usually Shailaja goes to the office, but this week she is working at the home.
    - (a) but this week she is
    - (b) working at the home
    - (c) Usually Shailaja goes to the office
    - (d) No error

22. This record sound exactly like the band's previous one.
    - (a) This record sound
    - (b) exactly like the
    - (c) band's previous one
    - (d) No error

**23.** The mango tree in my garden was loaded with fruit.
(a) The mango tree in
(b) my garden was
(c) loaded with fruit
(d) No error

**24.** Winning is not near as important as playing well.
(a) Winning is not near
(b) as important as
(c) playing well
(d) No error

**25.** It has taking almost a year for India to let its pessimism translate into fewer jobs.
(a) It has taking almost a year for
(b) India to let its pessimism
(c) Translate into fewer jobs
(d) No error

**Directions** (Q. Nos. 26 and 27) Choose the correct passive voice of the following sentences.

**26.** Who asked you to open the packet?
(a) By who you were asked to open this packet?
(b) By who have you been asked to open the packet?
(c) By whom were you asked to open the packet?
(d) By whom you were asked to open the packet?

**27.** We must endure what we cannot cure.
(a) What we cure must be endured.
(b) What cannot be cured must be endured.
(c) What cannot cured must endured.
(d) What could be cured must be endured.

**Directions** (Q. Nos. 28-30) Fill in the blanks by choosing the right option.

**28.** Prabha's ....... in athletics yielded rich dividends as she got a scholarship.
(a) performance     (b) defeat
(c) excellence      (d) behaviour

**29.** If Uday ...... thirsty, he would have drunk some water.
(a) was             (b) had been
(c) is              (d) would drink

**30.** She would have come if you ...... her.
(a) would invite
(b) had invited
(c) invited
(d) invite

**Directions** (Q. Nos. 31-35) Read the following article and fill in the blanks by choosing the correct option.

The ...(31)... towards marriage in urban India is turning turtle. The financial imperatives of modern, urban living demand that both ...(32)... should have a career. The crunch comes when the career woman demands an entity distinct from her husband and a measure of financial independence.

The woman's ...(33).... is that the man as the bread winner should be ...(34)... the household expenses, while what she earns is the jam over the bread and butter. And she gets to choose the ...(35).... of jam.

**31.** (a) demands        (b) economics
(c) attitude       (d) gratitude

**32.** (a) pairs          (b) partners
(c) couples        (d) spouse

**33.** (a) stance         (b) idea
(c) example        (d) thought

**34.** (a) shouldering   (b) bearing
(c) sharing   (d) dividing

**35.** (a) brand   (b) type
(c) colour   (d) mix

**Directions** (Q. Nos. 36-40) Read the following passage and answer the questions that follow.

**The Skater**

Aaron went in search for a place to skate. It felt totally bizarre to be walking down a narrow country road, his skateboard hanging from his fist. Ragged cattle eyed him, a slow crow sailed overhead, its call hanging like a streak of rust. Aaron's sneakers, dark blue and worn, looked wildly out of place. In Melbourne they'd looked fine, but out here in the sticks they looked as if they were a long way from home. What the hell, he thought; he liked the contrast.

Walking over a hill, Aaron saw that the thin bitumen road levelled out below to wind through the low land like a struggling eel. A spine of new, black tar ran down its centre, stopping abruptly where the road turned to gravel and disappeared amongst endless low hills and stony gullies. Aaron put his board down.

He loved to skate. It wasn't the tricks or the scene or the image; Aaron Knott just loved to be moving, even if it wasn't far, even if it wasn't fast. When he was cruising, thoughts didn't come and go or ricochet, they stayed away for a while, blunted and dormant. Aaron liked not to think. It made a change from thinking too much.

Five times he rode the strip, cold air flapping his pants and baggy windcheater. Five times he pushed back up the slope, arriving at the top hot and breathless. He stood for a minute, taking it all in: grey cloud, green ground, patches of sunlight, the lake.

**36.** It is possible to tell that the road on which Aaron was skating .............. .
(a) circled the lake
(b) wound through the countryside
(c) was completely sealed with bitumen
(d) was wider than he had expected

**37.** Where did Aaron skate?
(a) He skated past the lake several times.
(b) He skated as far as the low hills.
(c) He skated down the same hill repeatedly.
(d) He skated to the edge of the stony gullies.

**38.** In which of the following does the writer use a simile?
(a) 'Ragged cattle eyed him'.
(b) 'hanging like a streak of rust'.
(c) 'A spine of new, black tar'.
(d) 'the road turned to gravel'.

**39.** The word 'ricochet' as it is used in the passage, is closest in meaning to .........
(a) rebound   (b) dominate
(c) irritate   (d) react

**40.** The way that Aaron's sneakers are described suggests that Aaron ..........
(a) was surprised when he saw how worn out the sneakers were
(b) was embarrassed to wear the sneakers now that he was in the country
(c) thought the sneakers were too old and it was time to replace them
(d) enjoyed wearing the sneakers because they made him feel different

# 2 Marks Questions

**41.** Match the words given in List I with their antonyms given in List II.

| List I | List II |
|--------|---------|
| A. Exodus | 1. Advance |
| B. Timorous | 2. Convenient |
| C. Cumbersome | 3. Bold |
| D. Retreat | 4. Influx |

**Codes**

|     | A | B | C | D |
|-----|---|---|---|---|
| (a) | 4 | 3 | 1 | 2 |
| (b) | 2 | 3 | 1 | 4 |
| (c) | 3 | 1 | 2 | 4 |
| (d) | 4 | 3 | 2 | 1 |

**42.** Which of the following sentences are in Passive voice?

A. Mukul has been punished by his teacher.

B. None saw her in the parlour.

C. It is hoped that Rajesh will pass.

D. Her sudden arrival surprised everyone.

**Codes**

(a) A, B and C     (b) B and D

(c) A and C     (d) B, C and D

**43.** Match the words given in List I with those given in List II to form appropriate collocations.

| List I | List II |
|--------|---------|
| A. Prime | 1. Table |
| B. Round | 2. Suspect |
| C. Close | 3. Victory |
| D. Landslide | 4. Knit |

**Codes**

|     | A | B | C | D |     |     | A | B | C | D |
|-----|---|---|---|---|-----|-----|---|---|---|---|
| (a) | 2 | 1 | 3 | 4 |     | (b) | 2 | 1 | 4 | 3 |
| (c) | 4 | 1 | 2 | 3 |     | (d) | 3 | 2 | 1 | 4 |

**44.** Which of the following statements have the correct use of tenses?

A. Before she comes, the train will depart.

B. India had won freedom in 1947.

C. Metro trains run on this track every 5 minutes.

D. Why is Natasha cooking food today?

**Codes**

(a) A and B

(b) B and C

(c) B, C and D

(d) C and D

**45.** Match the words given in List I with their synonyms given in List II.

| List I | List II |
|--------|---------|
| A. Wicked | 1. Insignificant |
| B. Crooked | 2. Dissolute |
| C. Utterly | 3. Zigzag |
| D. Trivial | 4. Completely |

**Codes**

|     | A | B | C | D |
|-----|---|---|---|---|
| (a) | 2 | 3 | 4 | 1 |
| (b) | 1 | 2 | 3 | 4 |
| (c) | 4 | 3 | 2 | 1 |
| (d) | 3 | 2 | 1 | 4 |

**46.** Which of the following statements are true?

A. The Definite Article 'The' is used before the name of some countries.

B. 'Entirely' and 'Abroad' are adverbs.

C. 'Take' collocates properly with 'Chances'.

D. 'An' is used with 'University'.

**Codes**

(a) A, B and C

(b) B, C and D

(c) A and B

(d) C and D

**47.** Choose the uncountable nouns from the words listed in the box.

| | |
|---|---|
| Advice | Jargon |
| Loaf | Fuel |
| Particle | Nuisance |
| House | Shelf |

(a) Advice, Loaf and Nuisance
(b) Advice, Jargon, Fuel and Nuisance
(c) Fuel and Nuisance
(d) Jargon and Nuisance

**48.** Complete the following idioms by matching the words/phrases given in the List I with those given in List II.

| | List I | | List II |
|---|---|---|---|
| A. | Steal | 1. | own trumpet |
| B. | Blow your | 2. | the show |
| C. | To feather | 3. | oil on troubled waters |
| D. | To pour | 4. | one's nest |

**Codes**

|  | A | B | C | D | |  | A | B | C | D |
|---|---|---|---|---|---|---|---|---|---|---|
| (a) | 2 | 1 | 3 | 4 | | (b) | 3 | 2 | 4 | 1 |
| (c) | 2 | 1 | 4 | 3 | | (d) | 4 | 3 | 2 | 1 |

**49.** The following paragraph consists of six sentences.

The first and sixth sentences are labelled as $S_1$ and $S_6$ respectively. The middle four sentences have been jumbled up. These are labelled P, Q, R and S. Find out the proper order of the four sentences and select the correct option accordingly.

$S_1$. Some of the biggest and most important projects in the world have involved building bridges.

P. Bridges are crucial links that carry cars, trucks and trains across bodies of water, mountain gorges or other roads.

Q. Bridge collapses can be tragic events, leading to loss of life and serious property damage.

R. The best way to present these accidents is to understand why bridges collapse in the first place.

S. That's why bridge engineers, designers and builders must always take their jobs very seriously.

$S_6$. Understanding bridge collapses can lead to major changes in the design, construction and safety of future building projects.

**Codes**
(a) PQRS      (b) SRQP
(c) PQSR      (d) RQPS

**50.** Which of the following sentences are grammatically correct and meaningful?

A. One should be true to one's words.
B. There are hundreds of partially built houses in this colonies.
C. The students enjoyed themselves in summer vacations.
D. He was determined to avenge the death for his older brother.

**Codes**
(a) A and B
(b) C and D
(c) Only C
(d) Only B

# PRACTICE SET 02

## 1 Mark Questions

**1.** Which of the following is an uncountable noun?
 (a) Cliffhanger
 (b) Termite
 (c) Ode
 (d) Poetry

**Directions** (Q. Nos. 2 and 3) Choose the odd one out from the following.

**2.** (a) intermittently
 (b) constantly
 (c) unceasingly
 (d) continually

**3.** (a) Alluring
 (b) Simplistic
 (c) Condensed
 (d) Concede

**4.** Read the following paragraph.
 Dark clouds moved swiftly across the sky blotting out the sun. With no further warning, great cracks of thunder and flashes of lightning disturbed the morning's calm. Fortunately, the deckhands had already tied everything securely in place and closed all portholes and hatches or we would have lost our gear to the fury of wind and water. On the basis of your inference, state which of the following statements is false.
 (a) The storm was unexpected
 (b) The storm had been prepared for
 (c) It was windy
 (d) It was cloudy

**Directions** (Q. Nos. 5 and 6) Choose the correct option for the underlined word in each sentence.

**5.** Many people have pointed out the harmful effects that a working mother may have on the family, yet there are many <u>salutary</u> effects as well.
 Salutary means ......... .
 (a) well-known (b) beneficial
 (c) hurtful (d) side-effects

**6.** During their training, police officers must respond to <u>simulated</u> emergencies in preparation for dealing with real ones.
 Simulated means ......... .
 (a) made-up (b) mild
 (c) actual (d) real

**Directions** (Q. Nos. 7-12) Identify the part of the sentence that contains an error. In case, there is no error choose option (d) 'No error' as your answer.

**7.** The new law is too stringent; it will be neither respected or obeyed.
 (a) The new law is too stringent;
 (b) it will be neither be
 (c) respected or obeyed
 (d) No error

**8.** According to Hume, it is not logic and reasoning that determine our actions, but emotion.
 (a) According to Hume, it is not logic
 (b) and reasoning that determine
 (c) out actions, but emotion
 (d) No error

9. The four first boys will be given the chance to participate at national level.
   (a) The four first boys
   (b) will be given the chance to
   (c) participate at natural level
   (d) No error

10. The presence of strong feeling, the cause of which is not fully understood, always has the effect of making we human beings uneasy.
   (a) The presence of strong feeling, the cause of which
   (b) is not fully understood, always has the effect of
   (c) making we human beings uneasy
   (d) No error

11. Navneet didn't run good enough to qualify for the race.
   (a) Navneet didn't run good
   (b) enough to qualify
   (c) for the race
   (d) No error

12. The match hadn't hardly begun when it started raining.
   (a) The match hadn't
   (b) hardly begun
   (c) when it started raining
   (d) No error

13. Choose the adjective/s from the following.
   (a) Paisley
   (b) Canine
   (c) Theoretical
   (d) Both (b) and (c)

14. Choose the option that collocates properly.
   (a) undertake suicide
   (b) blow up in tears
   (c) vaguely remember
   (d) wave feverishly

**Directions** (Q. Nos. 15-19) Fill in the blanks by choosing the correct words from the given options.

15. If I ......... the problem to my cousin, Mintoo, he'll be happy to help me.
   (a) explain          (b) explained
   (c) will explain     (d) explains

16. If you ......... a red card, you can't play in the rest of the game.
   (a) gets             (b) will get
   (c) get              (d) got

17. What would you say if he ......... you for a date?
   (a) asks             (b) asked
   (c) would ask        (d) shall ask

18. I'm not interested in the actors. I always choose a film for its ......... .
   (a) special effects  (b) trailer
   (c) special affects  (d) space effects

19. We regret ......... inform you that you have not been admitted ......... our Ph.D programme.
   (a) to, too (b) for, to (c) to, to   (d) to, in

20. Rearrange the parts (P, Q, R and S) given below to produce a correct sentence.
   Nearly all
   P. man's character,
   Q. men can stand adversity,
   R. give him power
   S. but if you want to test a
   (a) QSPR (b) QRPS (c) PRQS (d) PRSQ

21. Fill in the blanks with appropriate adjectives.
   She were a .......... , white dress at her .......... wedding.
   (a) beautiful, thrift
   (b) ugly, expensive
   (c) beautiful, extravagant
   (d) beautiful, rubbish

**Directions** (Q. Nos. 22 and 23) Choose the correct indirect speech of the given sentences.

**22.** She said, "I had lived in five cities by the age of ten."

   (a) She said that she had lived in five cities by the age of ten.

   (b) She says that she had lived in five cities by the age of ten.

   (c) She said that she lived in five cities by the age of ten.

   (d) She said that she was living of five cities by the age of ten.

**23.** Nupur said, "I told Deepak to email you three days ago."

   (a) Nupur said that she told Deepak to email me three days ago.

   (b) Nupur said that she had told Deepak to email me three days before.

   (c) Nupur said that she told Deepak to email me three days before.

   (d) Nupur says that she had told Deepak to email me three days past.

**Directions** (Q. Nos. 24 and 25) Choose the correct passive voice of the following sentences.

**24.** Someone sent her a cheque for ₹10,000.

   (a) She was sent a cheque for ₹10,000 by someone.

   (b) She had been sent a cheque for ₹10,000.

   (c) She was being sent a cheque for ₹10,000.

   (d) She was sent a cheque for ₹10,000.

**25.** They will send her away to school.

   (a) She will being sent away to school.

   (b) She will be sent away to school.

   (c) She will have been sent away to school.

   (d) She would have been sent away to school.

**Directions** (Q. Nos. 26 and 27) Choose the correct antonym of the following.

**26.** Enraged

   (a) Pleased        (b) Livid

   (c) Aggravated     (d) Infuriated

**27.** Sporadic

   (a) Fake           (b) Scattered

   (c) Genuine       (d) Frequent

**28.** Choose the most appropriate response for the following.

Rohan : Pass me the book lying on your table.

Sohan : .........

   (a) You can have it!

   (b) Give me a break.

   (c) Take it on your own.

   (d) Here you are!

**Directions** (Q. Nos. 29 and 30) Choose the correct one word substitution for the following.

**29.** A man who is womanish in his habits.

   (a) Feminine      (b) Effeminate

   (c) Epicure        (d) Egotist

**30.** A group of worshippers

   (a) Congregation     (b) Convocation

   (c) Caravan        (d) Cache

**Directions** (Q. Nos. 31-35) Complete the following passage by filling the blanks.

London is the capital city of England situated on the bank of ...**(31)**... River Thames. It is an odd and ...**(32)**... city with many famous buildings, parks and places of interest to visit. Many tourists go to the Buckingham Palace, where the Queen lives, as it is one of the most recognisable places in the city.

London is also a multicultural city with people from all over the world. Hundreds of different languages are spoken and you can find a wide range of ...(33)... to eat and enjoy. Many international festivals are also celebrated ...(34)... the year in this ...(35)... global city.

31. (a) a     (b) an
    (c) the     (d) No article

32. (a) histronic     (b) hysteric
    (c) historic     (d) historical

33. (a) cuisine     (b) cuisines
    (c) menu     (d) menus

34. (a) throughout     (b) through
    (c) around     (d) in

35. (a) truthfully     (b) truly
    (c) purely     (d) pluraly

**Directions** (Q. Nos. 36-40) Read the following passage and answer the questions that follow.

The United Nations Fourth World Women's Conference had a colourful start at Beijing on September 4th. This is the century's most crucial conference which aimed at changing the status quo of women's lives characterised by inequality.

In a preliminary session, Ms Aung San Suu Kyi, the Nobel Peace Prize winner said that expanding women's power will bring greater peace and tolerance to the world.

"It is not the prerogative of men alone to bring light to this world. Women with their capacity for compassion and self-sacrifice, with their courage and perseverance, have done much to dissipate the darkness of intolerance and hate", said Ms Suu Kyi.

In the afternoon session Ms Ayako Yamaguchi, a Japanese delegate, launched a petition against beauty pageants. "What right do men have to evaluate women in a few minutes? All women are beautiful. Beauty is something different for everyone", Ms Ayako Yamaguchi said.

"Beauty contests are used as trade and exploitation. The training is very vigorous but it is the organisers, not the women, who get the full benefit", said Ms Ranjana Bhargava. "After the competition, the women become trapped and the abuse and the bad things begin. The women are tainted; no one else will accept them."

36. The Women's World Conference was very important because ......... .
    (a) Ms Aung Suu Kyi has just been awarded the prestigious Nobel Peace Prize
    (b) Ms Aung Suu Kyi was taking part in the conference
    (c) its main purpose was to change inequalities between men and women
    (d) it was to protest against beauty contests

37. Which of the following is not true regarding the statement of Ms Aung Suu Kyi?
    (a) Women also can bring greater peace to the world.
    (b) Men cannot claim they have done more for peace.
    (c) Women have the capacity for compassion and sacrifice.
    (d) Men have done nothing to dissipate ignorance.

38. The statement "Beauty is something different for everyone", means that ......... .
    (a) beauty is certainly different from ugliness
    (b) beauty cannot be defined adequately
    (c) beautiful women do not mingle with other women
    (d) each woman is beautiful

**39.** Antonym of 'prerogative' is ......... .

(a) authority      (b) advantage

(c) exemption      (d) obligation

**40.** What was the main emphasis in Ms Ayako Yamaguchi's argument?

(a) Men have no right to judge women.

(b) Men should be given more time to evaluate women.

(c) All women are beautiful in a way.

(d) Beauty contests are not necessary.

# 2 Marks Questions

**41.** Complete the idioms by matching words given in List I with those given in List II.

| | List I | | List II |
|---|---|---|---|
| A. | Better late | 1. | yourself together |
| B. | Go back to | 2. | than never |
| C. | Pull | 3. | the drawing board |
| D. | Under | 4. | the weather |

**Codes**

|   | A | B | C | D |   | A | B | C | D |
|---|---|---|---|---|---|---|---|---|---|
| (a) | 2 | 3 | 4 | 1 | (b) | 3 | 1 | 2 | 4 |
| (c) | 4 | 3 | 1 | 2 | (d) | 2 | 3 | 1 | 4 |

**42.** Which of the following sentences are in Passive voice?

A. Jayanti has been asked to make a speech at the meeting.

B. Tarun was looked after by his aunt.

C. A dangerous dog attacked Roopali.

D. They called off the meeting.

**Codes**

(a) A, B and C      (b) B and C

(c) C and D      (d) A and B

**43.** Match the words in List I to those given in List II to form appropriate collocations.

| | List I | | List II |
|---|---|---|---|
| A. | Start | 1. | Confidence |
| B. | Set out on | 2. | A Journey |
| C. | Give in | 3. | Work |
| D. | Consumer | 4. | Your homework |

**Codes**

|   | A | B | C | D |   | A | B | C | D |
|---|---|---|---|---|---|---|---|---|---|
| (a) | 3 | 2 | 1 | 4 | (b) | 4 | 1 | 2 | 3 |
| (c) | 3 | 2 | 4 | 1 | (d) | 1 | 2 | 3 | 4 |

**44.** In the following question is given a statement followed by two assumptions numbered I and II. You have to consider the statement and the following assumptions and decide which of the assumptions is implicit in the statement.

Statement: Unemployment allowance should be given to all unemployed Indian youth above 18 years of age.

Assumptions

I. There are unemployed youth in India who need monetary support.

II. The government has sufficient funds to provide allowance to all unemployed youth.

(a) Only assumption I is implicit

(b) Only assumption II is implicit

(c) Either I or II is implicit

(d) Neither I or II is implicit

**Directions** (Q. Nos. 45 and 46) Each passage consist of six sentences. The first and sixth sentences are labelled as $S_1$ and $S_6$ respectively. The middle four sentences in each have been jumbled up. These are labelled P, Q, R, S. Find out the proper order for the four sentences and select the correct option accordingly.

**45.** $S_1$ In 1934, William Golding published a small volume of poems.

P During World War II (1939-45), he joined the Royal Navy and was present at the sinking of the Bismarck.

Q He returned to teaching in 1945 and gave it up in 1962, and is now a full time writer.

R In 1939, he married and started teaching at Bishop Wordsworth school in Salisbury.

S At first, his novels were not accepted.

$S_6$ But Lord of the flies, which came out in 1954, was welcomed as "a most absorbing and instructive tale."

The proper sequence should be

(a) RPQS      (b) RPSQ
(c) SRPQ      (d) SQPR

**46.** $S_1$ Ghana is a country is Western Africa.

P Its proximity to the equator makes its climate hot.

Q It is surrounded by Cote d'Ivoir in the West, Togo in the East and Burkina Faso in the North.

R Ghana has abundant natural resources.

S To its South lies the Gulf of Guinea.

$S_6$ It is famous for being Africa's second largest producer of gold and the world's largest producer of cocoa beans.

(a) PQRS      (b) PRQS
(c) QSPR      (d) SRQP

**47.** Which of the following sentences have the correct use of tenses?

A. The doors are going to be locked at 10 o'clock.

B. I'll leave as soon as the babysitter is arriving.

C. If we had a garden, we could have a cat.

D. I will come home as soon as I have finish my work.

**Codes**

(a) Only B      (b) Only C
(c) C and D      (d) A and C

**48.** Match the one word substitutions given in List I with the things they are related to given in List II.

| List I | | List II | |
|---|---|---|---|
| A. | Neocracy | 1. | Sound |
| B. | Bale | 2. | Government |
| C. | Homicide | 3. | Bundle |
| D. | Creak | 4. | Murder |

**Codes**

| | A | B | C | D | | A | B | C | D |
|---|---|---|---|---|---|---|---|---|---|
| (a) | 2 | 3 | 1 | 4 | (b) | 3 | 1 | 2 | 4 |
| (c) | 2 | 3 | 4 | 1 | (d) | 1 | 3 | 2 | 4 |

**49.** Match the modals given in List I with their uses given in List II.

| List I | | List II | |
|---|---|---|---|
| A. | Can | 1. | Obligation |
| B. | Ought to | 2. | Ability |
| C. | May | 3. | Intention |
| D. | Will | 4. | Permission |

**Codes**

| | A | B | C | D | | A | B | C | D |
|---|---|---|---|---|---|---|---|---|---|
| (a) | 2 | 1 | 3 | 4 | (b) | 4 | 3 | 2 | 1 |
| (c) | 2 | 1 | 4 | 3 | (d) | 1 | 3 | 2 | 4 |

**50.** Which of the following sentences are grammatically correct and meaningful?

A. I am understanding you.

B. This cake tastes wonderful.

C. Tara is studying history in Delhi University.

D. Have you met ever Priyanshi?

**Codes**

(a) A and B      (b) B and C
(c) A, B and C      (d) Only C

# ANSWERS

## Chapter 1   Parts of Speech

| | | | | | | | | | |
|---|---|---|---|---|---|---|---|---|---|
| **1.** (c) | **2.** (b) | **3.** (d) | **4.** (c) | **5.** (d) | **6.** (a) | **7.** (b) | **8.** (d) | **9.** (b) | **10.** (b) |
| **11.** (b) | **12.** (a) | **13.** (b) | **14.** (c) | **15.** (c) | **16.** (b) | **17.** (d) | **18.** (c) | **19.** (a) | **20.** (b) |
| **21.** (d) | **22.** (c) | **23.** (c) | **24.** (a) | **25.** (d) | **26.** (b) | **27.** (c) | **28.** (d) | **29.** (d) | **30.** (a) |
| **31.** (b) | **32.** (a) | **33.** (b) | **34.** (d) | **35.** (d) | **36.** (c) | **37.** (b) | **38.** (d) | **39.** (c) | **40.** (d) |
| **41.** (d) | **42.** (a) | **43.** (b) | **44.** (c) | **45.** (a) | **46.** (d) | **47.** (b) | **48.** (c) | **49.** (b) | **50.** (d) |
| **51.** (a) | **52.** (c) | **53.** (d) | **54.** (c) | **55.** (a) | **56.** (b) | **57.** (d) | **58.** (b) | **59.** (a) | **60.** (c) |
| **61.** (b) | **62.** (c) | **63.** (c) | **64.** (a) | | | | | | |

## Chapter 2   Subject-Verb Agreement

| | | | | | | | | | |
|---|---|---|---|---|---|---|---|---|---|
| **1.** (b) | **2.** (b) | **3.** (a) | **4.** (a) | **5.** (b) | **6.** (b) | **7.** (a) | **8.** (b) | **9.** (c) | **10.** (c) |
| **11.** (b) | **12.** (c) | **13.** (b) | **14.** (d) | **15.** (c) | **16.** (b) | **17.** (a) | **18.** (a) | **19.** (c) | **20.** (a) |
| **21.** (d) | | | | | | | | | |

## Chapter 3   Tenses

| | | | | | | | | | |
|---|---|---|---|---|---|---|---|---|---|
| **1.** (a) | **2.** (c) | **3.** (c) | **4.** (b) | **5.** (b) | **6.** (d) | **7.** (d) | **8.** (a) | **9.** (c) | **10.** (b) |
| **11.** (a) | **12.** (b) | **13.** (b) | **14.** (b) | **15.** (a) | **16.** (c) | **17.** (b) | **18.** (a) | **19.** (c) | **20.** (b) |
| **21.** (d) | **22.** (b) | **23.** (b) | **24.** (a) | **25.** (b) | **26.** (c) | | | | |

## Chapter 4   Clauses and Conditionals

| | | | | | | | | | |
|---|---|---|---|---|---|---|---|---|---|
| **1.** (b) | **2.** (c) | **3.** (c) | **4.** (d) | **5.** (a) | **6.** (b) | **7.** (c) | **8.** (a) | **9.** (d) | **10.** (a) |
| **11.** (c) | **12.** (b) | **13.** (c) | **14.** (d) | **15.** (d) | **16.** (c) | **17.** (b) | **18.** (d) | **19.** (c) | **20.** (a) |
| **21.** (b) | **22.** (d) | **23.** (b) | **24.** (d) | **25.** (b) | | | | | |

## Chapter 5   Collocations

| | | | | | | | | | |
|---|---|---|---|---|---|---|---|---|---|
| **1.** (d) | **2.** (c) | **3.** (b) | **4.** (d) | **5.** (a) | **6.** (b) | **7.** (a) | **8.** (b) | **9.** (c) | **10.** (c) |
| **11.** (d) | **12.** (b) | **13.** (c) | **14.** (d) | **15.** (c) | **16.** (b) | **17.** (a) | **18.** (b) | **19.** (d) | **20.** (c) |
| **21.** (d) | **22.** (c) | **23.** (b) | **24.** (c) | **25.** (a) | **26.** (d) | **27.** (c) | | | |

## Chapter 6   Active/Passive Voice

| | | | | | | | | | |
|---|---|---|---|---|---|---|---|---|---|
| **1.** (b) | **2.** (d) | **3.** (b) | **4.** (c) | **5.** (d) | **6.** (a) | **7.** (d) | **8.** (c) | **9.** (c) | **10.** (a) |
| **11.** (b) | **12.** (d) | **13.** (a) | **14.** (a) | **15.** (c) | **16.** (b) | **17.** (c) | **18.** (d) | **19.** (d) | **20.** (c) |
| **21.** (a) | **22.** (b) | **23.** (c) | **24.** (d) | **25.** (b) | **26.** (i) (a) (ii) (c) (iii) (c) | | | | |

## Chapter 7  Direct/Indirect Speech

| 1. (a) | 2. (d) | 3. (c) | 4. (b) | 5. (d) | 6. (c) | 7. (d) | 8. (a) | 9. (a) | 10. (a) |
|---|---|---|---|---|---|---|---|---|---|
| 11. (b) | 12. (a) | 13. (b) | 14. (b) | 15. (d) | 16. (b) | 17. (d) | 18. (a) | | |

## Chapter 8  Jumbled Sentences

| 1. (a) | 2. (b) | 3. (c) | 4. (d) | 5. (b) | 6. (d) | 7. (c) | 8. (a) | 9. (a) | 10. (c) |
|---|---|---|---|---|---|---|---|---|---|
| 11. (b) | 12. (b) | 13. (c) | 14. (b) | 15. (a) | 16. (d) | 17. (c) | 18. (a) | 19. (c) | 20. (c) |
| 21. (b) | 22. (b) | 23. (b) | 24. (c) | | | | | | |

## Chapter 9  Synonyms and Antonyms

| 1. (b) | 2. (c) | 3. (b) | 4. (d) | 5. (a) | 6. (d) | 7. (c) | 8. (a) | 9. (d) | 10. (c) |
|---|---|---|---|---|---|---|---|---|---|
| 11. (a) | 12. (d) | 13. (b) | 14. (b) | 15. (c) | 16. (c) | 17. (a) | 18. (a) | 19. (b) | 20. (a) |
| 21. (b) | 22. (d) | 23. (b) | 24. (d) | 25. (b) | 26. (c) | 27. (c) | 28. (d) | 29. (d) | 30. (c) |

## Chapter 10  One Word Substitutions

| 1. (d) | 2. (c) | 3. (b) | 4. (d) | 5. (c) | 6. (a) | 7. (b) | 8. (c) | 9. (d) | 10. (c) |
|---|---|---|---|---|---|---|---|---|---|
| 11. (c) | 12. (d) | 13. (d) | 14. (a) | 15. (c) | 16. (d) | 17. (a) | 18. (b) | 19. (d) | |

## Chapter 11  Idioms and Phrases

| 1. (c) | 2. (b) | 3. (d) | 4. (d) | 5. (b) | 6. (a) | 7. (a) | 8. (c) | 9. (b) | 10. (b) |
|---|---|---|---|---|---|---|---|---|---|
| 11. (a) | 12. (b) | 13. (d) | 14. (b) | 15. (d) | 16. (c) | 17. (c) | 18. (c) | 19. (a) | 20. (d) |
| 21. (b) | 22. (d) | 23. (c) | 24. (c) | 25. (d) | 26. (a) | 27. (b) | 28. (d) | 29. (a) | |

## Chapter 12  Cloze Test

| 1. (c) | 2. (a) | 3. (b) | 4. (b) | 5. (c) | 6. (b) | 7. (d) | 8. (b) | 9. (a) | 10. (d) |
|---|---|---|---|---|---|---|---|---|---|
| 11. (a) | 12. (b) | 13. (a) | 14. (d) | 15. (a) | 16. (a) | 17. (d) | 18. (c) | 19. (d) | 20. (a) |
| 21. (c) | 22. (c) | 23. (b) | 24. (a) | 25. (a) | 26. (i) (a), (ii) (d), (iii) (c), (iv) (d), (v) (c) | | | | |

27. (i) (d), (ii) (c), (iii) (b), (iv) (d), (v) (c)          28. (i) (c), (ii) (a), (iii) (a), (iv) (a), (v) (b)

29. (i) (a), (ii) (b), (iii) (c), (iv) (d), (v) (a)

## Chapter 13  Reading Comprehension

| 1. (b) | 2. (d) | 3. (a) | 4. (a) | 5. (b) | 6. (c) | 7. (c) | 8. (d) | 9. (a) | 10. (b) |
|---|---|---|---|---|---|---|---|---|---|
| 11. (a) | 12. (c) | 13. (d) | 14. (c) | 15. (a) | 16. (b) | 17. (b) | 18. (b) | 19. (a) | 20. (b) |
| 21. (a) | 22. (d) | 23. (b) | 24. (d) | 25. (d) | 26. (b) | 27. (d) | 28. (a) | 29. (b) | 30. (d) |
| 31. (b) | 32. (d) | | | | | | | | |

## Chapter 14   Writing Skills

| | | | | | | | | | |
|---|---|---|---|---|---|---|---|---|---|
| **1.** (c) | **2.** (b) | **3.** (a) | **4.** (d) | **5.** (a) | **6.** (b) | **7.** (d) | **8.** (a) | **9.** (c) | **10.** (b) |
| **11.** (b) | **12.** (c) | **13.** (a) | **14.** (d) | **15.** (a) | **16.** (d) | **17.** (b) | **18.** (c) | **19.** (a) | **20.** (b) |
| **21.** (b) | **22.** (d) | **23.** (c) | **24.** (b) | **25.** (b) | **26.** (d) | **27.** (d) | **28.** (c) | **29.** (c) | **30.** (c) |
| **31.** (c) | **32.** (a) | **33.** (b) | **34.** (d) | **35.** (a) | **36.** (d) | **37.** (a) | **38.** (c) | **39.** (b) | **40.** (a) |
| **41.** (b) | **42.** (a) | **43.** (c) | **44.** (b) | **45.** (d) | **46.** (b) | **47.** (d) | **48.** (a) | **49.** (b) | **50.** (d) |
| **51.** (c) | **52.** (d) | **53.** (a) | **54.** (b) | **55.** (a) | **56.** (d) | **57.** (c) | **58.** (a) | **59.** (b) | **60.** (a) |
| **61.** (c) | **62.** (d) | **63.** (b) | **64.** (b) | **65.** (b) | | | | | |

## Chapter 15   Communication Skills

| | | | | | | | | | |
|---|---|---|---|---|---|---|---|---|---|
| **1.** (c) | **2.** (b) | **3.** (d) | **4.** (b) | **5.** (a) | **6.** (a) | **7.** (c) | **8.** (a) | **9.** (d) | **10.** (c) |
| **11.** (c) | **12.** (d) | **13.** (b) | **14.** (b) | **15.** (a) | **16.** (b) | **17.** (b) | **18.** (d) | **19.** (d) | **20.** (a) |
| **21.** (b) | **22.** (d) | **23.** (c) | | | | | | | |

## Chapter 16   Verbal Ability

| | | | | | | | | | |
|---|---|---|---|---|---|---|---|---|---|
| **1.** (a) | **2.** (c) | **3.** (a) | **4.** (c) | **5.** (b) | **6.** (b) | **7.** (d) | **8.** (a) | **9.** (d) | **10.** (b) |
| **11.** (a) | **12.** (d) | **13.** (c) | **14.** (a) | **15.** (c) | **16.** (b) | **17.** (a) | **18.** (c) | **19.** (a) | **20.** (c) |
| **21.** (b) | **22.** (b) | **23.** (c) | **24.** (d) | **25.** (c) | | | | | |

## Practice Set-1

| | | | | | | | | | |
|---|---|---|---|---|---|---|---|---|---|
| **1.** (a) | **2.** (b) | **3.** (d) | **4.** (a) | **5.** (c) | **6.** (d) | **7.** (c) | **8.** (b) | **9.** (d) | **10.** (c) |
| **11.** (a) | **12.** (d) | **13.** (a) | **14.** (d) | **15.** (d) | **16.** (b) | **17.** (b) | **18.** (a) | **19.** (b) | **20.** (c) |
| **21.** (b) | **22.** (a) | **23.** (c) | **24.** (a) | **25.** (a) | **26.** (c) | **27.** (b) | **28.** (c) | **29.** (b) | **30.** (b) |
| **31.** (c) | **32.** (b) | **33.** (b) | **34.** (b) | **35.** (a) | **36.** (b) | **37.** (c) | **38.** (b) | **39.** (a) | **40.** (d) |
| **41.** (d) | **42.** (c) | **43.** (b) | **44.** (d) | **45.** (a) | **46.** (a) | **47.** (b) | **48.** (c) | **49.** (c) | **50.** (c) |

## Practice Set-2

| | | | | | | | | | |
|---|---|---|---|---|---|---|---|---|---|
| **1.** (d) | **2.** (a) | **3.** (d) | **4.** (a) | **5.** (b) | **6.** (a) | **7.** (c) | **8.** (d) | **9.** (a) | **10.** (c) |
| **11.** (a) | **12.** (a) | **13.** (d) | **14.** (c) | **15.** (a) | **16.** (c) | **17.** (c) | **18.** (a) | **19.** (c) | **20.** (a) |
| **21.** (c) | **22.** (a) | **23.** (b) | **24.** (d) | **25.** (b) | **26.** (a) | **27.** (d) | **28.** (d) | **29.** (b) | **30.** (a) |
| **31.** (c) | **32.** (c) | **33.** (b) | **34.** (a) | **35.** (b) | **36.** (c) | **37.** (d) | **38.** (b) | **39.** (d) | **40.** (c) |
| **41.** (d) | **42.** (d) | **43.** (c) | **44.** (a) | **45.** (a) | **46.** (c) | **47.** (d) | **48.** (c) | **49.** (c) | **50.** (b) |